CAL
PO

CALL THE POLICE
There's a Mad Man Around

A Memoir of
Life in the Met

Paul Byrne

Scratching Shed Publishing Ltd

Copyright © Paul Byrne 2024
All rights reserved
The moral right of the authors has been asserted
First published by Scratching Shed Publishing Ltd in 2024
Registered in England & Wales No. 6588772
Registered office: 47 Street Lane, Leeds, West Yorkshire. LS8 1AP
www.scratchingshedpublishing.co.uk
ISBN: 978-1739247690

Cover image: © Adobe Stock
Back cover images: © Stephen Norman Young

No part of this book may be reproduced or transmitted in any form or by any other means without the written permission of the publisher, except by a reviewer who wishes to quote brief passages in connection with a review written for insertion in a magazine, newspaper or broadcast.

Every effort has been made to obtain the necessary permissions with reference to copyright material, both illustrative and quoted. We apologise for any omissions in this respect and will be pleased to make the appropriate acknowledgements in any future edition.

A catalogue record for this book is available from the British Library.

Printed and bound in the UK
by TJ Books

Trecerus Industrial Estate, Padstow,
Cornwall PL28 8RW
www.tjbooks.co.uk

This book is dedicated to the women of Shepherd's Bush
who died in a burning building in 1995.

Contents

1. How it all Began 1
2. My First Arrest 14
3. Driving to a Different Beat 25
4. Night Time is the Right Time 37
5. Very Important People 43
6. Wannabe Detectives 49
7. You Don't Have to be Mad 58
8. A New Millennium 65
9. Dead People Everywhere 75
10. Call Me Sarge 85
11. Intestines All Over the Shop 98
12. Murder in Belgravia 111
13. Life's a Riot 119
14. Taken Into Custody 129
15. Worst Case Scenarios 142
16. Corruption Comes Home to Roost 150
17. Missing People 159
18. Surreal Times 167
19. Lies, Damn Lies 176
20. Downfall of an Online Satirist 181
21. Pulling the Pin on the Hand Grenade 189

'People sleep peacefully in their beds at night only because rough men stand ready to do violence on their behalf...'
– **George Orwell**

'The Police are the Public; the Public are the Police...'
– **Sir Robert Peel**

'We're the Sweeney, son, and we haven't had any dinner. You've kept us waiting, so unless you want a kicking you tell us where those photographs are...'
– *'**The Sweeney**'*

1

How It All Began – A Slap in the Face and Other Self-Defence Techniques

Wellingborough, Northamptonshire, is where I grew up. My parents lived there, so it made sense. I was schooled at Thomas Beckett Roman Catholic Upper, Northampton, where eventually I was asked to leave, having been captured dancing on a gantry when I ought to have been attending lessons.

Undeterred, I embarked on a course in philosophy and psychology at Middlesex Polytechnic, north London. Until, that is, I saw someone had written 'Philosophy Degrees' in marker on a campus toilet roll dispenser. So I washed my hands of that idea too, apparently on a downward spiral.

Two years working at Our Price Records followed (a period in which I refused to serve pop star Gloria Estefan) until, in 1993, I accidentally applied to join the Metropolitan Police Service, lured by an advert in the *London Evening Standard*.

The Met very kindly replied. Twice. Their first letter thanked me for my interest, but said they were not currently recruiting, wishing me every success in the future. The second also thanked me for writing and invited me to interview. I tossed a coin. Heads I'm going to be a copper; tails I'll carry on being a human being. Given the name of this book, you've likely guessed the outcome.

I was directed to attend Paddington Green Police Station, a nick that lay on the Edgeware Road, nestled within the shadow of the Euston Road overpass. At the time, it was a high-security police station, used to house IRA prisoners. I hoped that my Irish surname wouldn't lead to any awkward mix-ups.

I didn't know much about the police, so researched what I could. I did clock how one recruitment poster showing a white policeman chasing a black guy was there to test our perceptions. The latter was a police officer too, acting undercover. It turned out that both were chasing an actual villain together. Clever stuff.

I'd also watched *The Bill* religiously, *Hill Street Blues* before it, and on the application form pointed to the Estefan-gate incident as evidence that I was no stranger to conflict.

Arriving in plenty of time, I joined a long line of skinny white men in cheap suits seated outside rooms with light bulbs above their doors, feeling less like I was at a police station than an estate agency stag do in Amsterdam. We were, though, being assessed. Any hint of subversion and you'd be gone. Fortunately, I'd given my *New Musical Express* to a homeless person outside the station. If the recruitment team saw that, they'd think I was left-wing.

Then I set about carefully filling in a security questionnaire in which I was asked to confirm that I had never engaged in terrorism or indulged in any acts intended to undermine the economic security of the United Kingdom, questions I'd be asked every ten years during my eventual period of service; yes/no tick-box exercises being a failsafe way to prevent terrorist infiltration.

Soon, a bulb turned green and I knocked in a commanding yet respectful manner. Summoned, I sat before a Detective Chief

Inspector and uniformed Superintendent. It now felt very real indeed. I was one step closer to becoming the guy in *Hill Street Blues* who growled and lived in a bin.

And this DCI sure had presence. On his third wife by the look of it, he looked as if he'd spent a night on the whisky recruiting snouts in an East End snooker club, and had slept in his suit. My deduction skills, however, needed fine-tuning. It turned out this particular detective was on secondment to Human Resources, while studying towards a PHD in resource management.

The Superintendent told me to sit down, the sort of man, I imagined, who would enjoy being saluted. They asked me why I wanted to join the force. I told them that I loved the recruitment poster and now felt like crying having realised my prejudices. The DCI seemed to like my willingness to admit to emotions, but the Superintendent looked ready to punch me in the glasses.

'Come on, be honest. What's driving you?' he insisted.

'I want to help people less fortunate than myself and I care about small animals,' I replied, or words to that effect.

After a further half-hour grilling, I was ordered to leave by another door and sit in line with a further row of skinny white men in cheap suits, a couple of whom were later asked to leave when found to have criminal records. Trying to hide that from the police takes cahoonas, but fair play to them for giving it a go.

Before long, a kindly woman took me to a sideroom and said I'd been accepted as a probationary police constable. As I thanked her and went on my way, her eyes seemed to well with pity.

I however was on cloud nine. I had got the job – and not just any job. I was going to be a real life policeman! After punching the air in delight, I snatched back my *New Musical Express* from the homeless guy and raced across London to tell my girlfriend who, I now discovered, had run off with another man.

So I went to sit in my bedsit instead.

On 19 September 1994, I arrived at the Met Police training school to begin an eighteen-week residential programme among around 100 other such students. A fresh intake arrived every five weeks, with three or four such courses running at any one time.

My time in Hendon, the venue, would change me in so many ways. When I arrived, I was a liberal music-loving bookworm. I still was when I left, but they'd given me a silly hat and a different way of seeing the world. We became soaked in groupthink, an understanding it was us against them, the undefined 'others' we would rage against. A tight-knit team of new constables, we came to rely on each other to last the course.

It all began on a crisp Sunday morning. The tube en route had been full of crop-haired men heading for the same destination who seemed way more confident and savvy than I felt. Outside the station, bag on pavement, my bewilderment must have been obvious to the police trainers who called me over to a minibus and ticked my name off their clipboard list. I found myself sitting next to an honest-looking chap who, like me, was destined for F Class, part of Green Intake, the eighth such group of the year so far. Upon graduation, this same guy was destined to be posted to the furthest reaches of east London where, in the not-too-distant, he would be arrested for drink-driving and enter into a fistfight with the arresting officers from Essex Constabulary.

Anyway, for now we were driven to the main training school site, a collection of tower blocks, low rise classrooms, gyms and food halls with police officers everywhere you looked. I checked my pockets to make sure I had nothing on me I shouldn't have. The Met's use of Stop and Search was notorious back then.

The F Class lead instructor was a traffic sergeant with an inflated ego and moustache that didn't quite give the impression he thought, and he was assisted by a couple of doughy Constables we were instructed to address as 'Staff'.

Later that day we swore an oath to the Queen and were now crown servants. I felt my Republican sympathies burning within my soul, so only mouthed the words, fingers crossed behind my back. Radical. I was glad my new pal didn't notice. He looked the sort to knock a person out for disrespecting the monarchy.

Having signed lots of bits of paper, we were then issued with various bits of uniform and equipment before being sent to our basic but clean rooms, each with a sink that proved particularly handy for the gentlemen. After which, we were given the rest of the day to get to know each other in the Peel Bar which, far from having anything to do with legendary indie music DJ John Peel, was named in honour of a crusty old chap from a previous century.

I'm joking. Sir Robert Peel, of course, was the founder of the Metropolitan Police Service and his statue was a centrepiece of the training estate. One night, persons unknown saw fit to jam an inflatable sex doll under his arm. A notable talking point for the visiting Japanese senior police officers the following morning.

That's how it was, some recruits less raw than others. Those with a military background had the bearing and haircuts to comfortably slip into the discipline of uniformed service. Others boasted of service as Special Constables. Those such as myself, young and mostly from outside London, were coated in naïvety, having little understanding of what lay in wait, other than vague thoughts of a blistering adventure stretching far down the yellow brick road. Or was I the only one who felt like that? I doubt our future fist-fighter fantasied about wearing ruby red slippers.

For me, there were sudden twinges of doubt, feelings of being ill-prepared, too young, too shy of the world, actually to become a copper, while a good few of the others talked about motorbikes and looked like they knew what to do in a betting shop.

I sat opposite one young woman who blushed when spoken to. She was the first person I encountered during my police career who would go on to be overwhelmed by it all, become consumed by despair. Tragically, she took her own life some years later.

Like so many others.

During those first two weeks, we were given basic instruction in all aspects of the Metropolitan Police Service. The Met remains proud of its illustrious history and is bitterly protective of its reputation. Scotland Yard has built a worldwide reputation of excellence in investigation, albeit often on the back of fictional detectives. Britain's police force, of which the Met is one quarter, remains one of the very few unarmed services in the world.

Its darker side would, for now, stay hidden. Hendon Training School, despite appearing big and scary to us fresh-faced recruits, was the soft side of policing. We were a world away from the horrors awaiting us... corruption lurking in corridors of power ... resentment of communities ... histories tarnished with conflict. The legacy of the miners' strike, suss laws, rioting, racism – all that seemed to be a different world. The horror of Hillsborough was still recent, general opinion still blaming the innocent souls who died that day. The police were the law and the default position was that we were never wrong.

I was the police, and the police was me.

Come weeks three and four, we were allowed onto the streets of London for a two-week attachment to the areas we would be working once we finished training, two-year probationary period postings on the emergency response teams, working earlies, lates and nights. Basically, thrown in at the deep end.

London was split into divisions, each represented by two letters. Every Police Constable (PC) had a three-figure shoulder number. I was posted to Shepherd's Bush, part of Hammersmith Division. FH. Foxtrot Hotel. Or Fucking Hard, as I liked to joke. And nobody laughed. Is a joke a joke if nobody laughs?

I was PC 410FH Byrne. I would be working with people who joined the police before my parents had met. They in turn would have had colleagues with connections to the war generation. Time is short. Life is short.

Six of us Green intakes went to Hammersmith, where we

spent our two weeks going around in police cars with real cops, experiencing the reality. Shepherd's Bush police station was just around the corner from Loftus Road, home of QPR football club.

This part of West London sits just beyond the nowadays gentrified streets of Notting Hill. In the 1990s, it was still full of genuinely local people. Shepherd's Bush Green was a focal point, populated with drug takers and incensed drunks. The Shepherd's Bush Empire – now the O2 – and massive Australasian drinking hole The Walkabout covered one side of the area. North along Wood Lane lay the BBC, its famous building in stark contrast to the White City Estate, a residential area notoriously hard to police, riven with poverty and social ills.

Following training school, we would be chaperoned by Street Duties Instructors for the first ten weeks, who would manage our development, a Sergeant and some experienced PCs. We'd sit in the backs of cars, be thrown around in vans and watch from afar as genuine emergencies were handled. I was enthralled, utterly overwhelmed by people and situations I had never experienced, and never would again outside that world. I felt a huge surge of adrenaline as we accelerated towards emergency calls, sirens shrieking, blue lights thudding overhead. I felt the madness of a busy shift, the officers' desperate attempts to keep decent people safe and lock up the bad guys.

And then one of us was killed on duty.

PC Matthew Parsonson was in my sister class at Hendon. We'd spoken a few times, shared beers in the Peel Bar. He had been posted to Stoke Newington for his two-week attachment. An urgent assistance call was received, sent whenever a police officer is in immediate danger. The car Matthew was in crashed en route to the scene, an impact that for Matthew proved fatal.

I was given the news in the canteen at Shepherd's Bush, along with a can of Coke. It wasn't intended as an uncaring gesture, just indicated how brutal the simple reality of policing can be.

Matthew had two young children and had served only three

weeks before his death. Twenty years later, a ceremony was held in his honour at Hendon. His two sons, grown-up now, were in attendance as we remembered their father.

Our return to Hendon was tempered with sadness, but we remained enthused by our experiences. I was determined to succeed and became utterly enthralled by the police experience. Maybe it was youth, but I don't remember imagining Matthew's death as my own. Youth can make us feel invincible.

I was however somewhat surprised to learn that our intake was earning less than previous newbies. We were the first not to receive Housing Allowance, a handy boost to the pay packet that helped with the rising cost of living in London. For me, this was not an issue, pulling in far more than I ever had at Our Price. Some of my peers though took umbrage and tempers frayed.

Nor did it help when the prior bunch mockingly waved their payslips at us, in homage to their predecessors waving wads of cash at striking miners. So strong was the mood of ill-feeling that outbreaks of disorder were prepared for. One balmy evening, the Territorial Support Group, aka riot police, were called to the training estate to be held in reserve. Yes, the police thought there was going to be a riot at the police training school.

By this time my class had bonded, standing together against a cruel world. Us against them. I hadn't expected 'them' to be other trainee police officers, but there you go. We soon knew each other well enough for nicknames. Coming up with one for a bloke who liked to masturbate sitting at a bar was easy enough. He'd been in the army, of course. Another lad's might have been 'Laptop' as he was a small PC, but they weren't invented then.

Away from sporadic outbreaks of disorder, training continued apace. Physicality was key. The PT instructors loved screaming and twisting people up in handcuffs; a bit like bondage parlour workers with warrant cards and no safe words. Each session was intended to push us to our physical limits and leave us with red welts on different parts of our body.

We were dressed in white T-shirts, surnames stencilled down one side so we could still be yelled at when uable to tell them our names, while busy being choked into submission perhaps. We were also put in height order. I was second tallest in the group and, as such, paired with Big Graham for matters of fitness and violence. He was known as Big Graham because he was big and his name was Graham – a heavyweight boxer built like a brick outhouse no-one had the bottle to call anything else. I was a slender ginger-haired dandy whose only experience of violence was being chased through Wellingborough town centre on a Saturday night due to being a slender ginger-haired dandy.

Unintentionally, Graham would batter the living shit out of me, struggling to understand how anyone could be so bad at fighting. A man without malice, he would later resign from the force fearing he would accidentally kill someone. An honourable decision indeed. I would have applauded, but he might have thought I was being sarcastic and got medieval on my ass.

We were often 'beasted', which had nothing to do with animal husbandry. It meant repeating activities until we had a bit of sick in our mouths, intended to test a trainee's mettle. Our class was once subjected to a 'double-beasting'. Getting changed after one session, the changing room door was suddenly flung open by an extraordinarily angry PTI who demanded to know who had called a female colleague a lesbian. Nobody was the answer. It would have been a remarkably stupid thing to do because she'd have kicked your head in.

The PTI was not satisfied with our denials, so 'beasted' us all over again. Most were in tears except for Ali, who lived within a different dimension. He just smiled. I do not need to describe the reaction of angry PTIs to a small chap smiling at such a time. Karma came when the accusatory PTI was sick across the senior officer's table at our leaving ball. Fit men are often unable to hold their drink, as I would later discover when threatened with death by a heavily intoxicated member of the Special Forces.

A key part of physical training was learning self-defence. As one of the only unarmed police services in the world, and before the general issue of body armour, this was quite a tall order.

To deal with agitated gentlemen, we were taught that a raised voice often does the trick. For the agitated chap with a knife, we were shown how to link our thumbs together to make a butterfly shape with our hands, apparently to protect the underside of our wrists while swiping said hands at the knife.

For really angry sorts with guns, we had somehow to lift our bodyweight onto their arms, throw ourselves to the floor and bring our elbows into forceful contact with the attacker's nose. This remained standard training for years until some smartarse in the medical profession advised that such action may lead to the nose cartilage being forced into the brain, leading to death.

In fact, training was constantly adapted to take into account new developments. Years later, we would gather in a gym to role-play legging it from a gunman in zig-zags. We literally practised running away. Then again I've never been shot, so it worked.

Classroom-based lessons took up most of our day however. Metropolitan Police officers are taught criminal law by cartoons. We were provided with notes illustrated by little drawings of people up to no good. One cartoon chap, 'Sprake', was used to instruct us in public order offences. He began his day by using some purple language to an elderly neighbour. By lunchtime, he was causing a row down the boozer. Come sundown, he was mounting an insurrection against the state apparatus. I blamed the parents, but Staff said it wasn't my place to judge and awarded me a C minus.

Having absorbed the 'toons, it was again time for role-playing, putting knowledge into action. Training school had an area that pretended to be the real world with roads, parked cars and a drill instructor's office where he practised his shouting. We would gather there to be briefed by Staff. One of us would be chosen to be a patrolling constable in a scenario of Staff's choosing. The rest of us would be goodies and baddies; a bit like playing 'war' at school only with the kids in glasses not having to be Germans.

The chosen PC had to deal with matters in police-prescribed fashion. Health and safety prevented use of unnecessary violence, or 'summary justice' as it is known in policing circles, so we just had to have pretend fights. I recall one with great fondness.

Big Graham was playing the suspect in a scene set in a gents toilet, where he wedged himself into a cubicle. Someone else played the part of toilet owner, demanding that Big Graham exit his premises forthwith. A refusal led to the police being called. Staff did not flesh out why it was being demanded that Graham should leave. Had he overstayed his welcome in some way?

Enter, stage right, another trainee.

Graham had been briefed to refuse to believe this copper was real, so the officer pushed his warrant card under the door to prove his ID, whereupon Graham flushed it down the bog. To this day, I've no idea what this scenario was meant to teach us.

That self-regarding Traffic Sergeant we met earlier, by the way, with the dodgy moustache, disappeared overnight and I would come to recognise this as a trait unique to people who had to line-manage me. He was replaced by a Detective Sergeant we'll call Dick. A DS teaching uniformed officers was highly unusual and led to rumours which, for litigation's sake, I intend to swerve.

Dick settled in straight away and took role-playing to new heights. One afternoon he summoned some of his old detective mates to facilitate a scenario for us, staged in the Peel Bar. I was chosen to participate, along with the smallest PC in the class. The scenario: a group of men were refusing to leave a bar, the 'actors' having got into role by drinking heavily throughout the morning. Method acting, if you will.

I followed my training to the letter and came into the pub wearing my big pointy helmet. Dick played the licensee and told me the group was very drunk and he had decided not to serve them anymore so as not to breach his responsibilities under the Licensing Act. I went over and formally introduced myself as a member of the constabulary. They each stepped forward and shook my hand, a twist I wasn't expecting but which seemed to amuse them. I stepped back and spoke to my colleague, smiling in a worryingly vacant fashion. We agreed they were drunk and that we ought to assist the landlord in getting rid of them. I again followed routine and attempted to lead the closest one out by the elbow. Then the pissed detectives got really carried away.

I took a right hiding as my oppo stood and made meticulous notes in his pocketbook. Dick called 'time' and helped to knock the dents out of my helmet. I nursed my injuries but reflected on how, while the detectives were beating me up, at least they hadn't been fitting innocent people up with residential burglaries.

I had made my first contribution to civil society.

Very early on, they told us that people accused of crimes could be taken to court. Who knew? Police officers would also have to go and explain to everyone there what had happened.

We had a day in pretend court at training school, taught by a solicitor who seemed surprised by our literacy levels. I told him I'd done six months of philosophy. 'There is only one thing a philosopher can be relied upon to do, and that is to contradict other philosophers,' he said. 'Oh, piss off,' I replied.

In those days, Magistrates were inclined to believe the word of a police officer. How mad is that?

We were shown how to present the most wooden of performances, banging on about 'proceeding in a northerly direction', and all that jazz. I always felt that conviction rates would be much increased if we were allowed greater artistic licence. We could break down in tears, for example, or point at the suspect and shouting, *'J'accuse!'*

Evenings saw the gentleman of F Class gather on the tenth floor of C Block, where we would study our cartoons and the ex-army chaps showed us feckless types how to iron our shirts and trousers properly. They also taught us how to ball our shoes, which isn't as painful as it sounds. Shoeing balls is much worse.

In preparation for our passing out parade, we had lessons in marching by a drill instructor in one of those shiny caps that cover the eyes. He also, inexplicably, dealt with lost property.

Each morning we'd line up in front of the Duty Inspector. He would strut up and down with the Drill Instructor bulging along behind him, stopping occasionally to look you up and down, say how shiny your shoes were or critique the crease in your trousers. Nobody cared, but as a disciplined service an exaggerated yawn wasn't deemed acceptable. Upset the Duty Inspector and you'd be kept behind marching up and down while the Drill Instructor bounced along next to you roaring in your ear.

It was very, very camp.

As was fairly standard back then, many new recruits were ex-services. One of F Class claimed to be an army captain until the real ex-soldiers worked out he wasn't, so he made his excuses and left. I believe he's an astronaut these days. The real ex-soldiers were quite good at marching, so we would have extra lessons with them before the bar opened. I asked one if he'd been in 'Nam, but he didn't know what I was talking about.

At the end of the course, the time came for us to demonstrate our marching skills at that passing out parade, friends and family invited, in which we stomped around in pouring rain to the Metropolitan Police Brass Band playing 'The Liberty Bell', by John Philip Sousa, which is best known, appropriately enough, as the theme tune to *Monty Python's Flying Circus*.

The time had come for something completely different...

My First Arrest – and How Team 3 Learned to Love Me

The next ten weeks were spent at Shepherd's Bush police station on a Street Duties course. It was designed as a gentle introduction to the more practical side of policing in which you were expected to make arrests, process traffic offences, patrol on foot and deal with sudden deaths, among other such tasks. Fitting up armed robbers would come later, I assumed.

We were given the same instructors as during our earlier two week attachment; those charmers who gave me the can of Coke.

These people were all volunteers, willing to engage with new officers – or get off with them in the pub after work. One regaled us with tales of personal omnipotence until we bowed in awe. He also offered to attend a post-mortem with us, the first time we had seen a dead body, let alone one chopped up by a doctor with an IQ higher than ours combined.

This guy spent some time preparing us for the experience. He spoke of the shock we might feel, outlined the sounds and smells we should expect. We could go in only when we were ready to do so, he said. It wouldn't be a problem if anyone wanted to stay outside. He would respect that decision, absolutely. And when the time came, he duly satisfied himself that we were as ready as we would ever be, led us through to the mortuary and fainted.

To begin with, each of us was paired with one instructor until, after a couple of weeks, being let loose. Firstly in pairs and then alone, on foot. The expectation was that we would generate work by way of issuing tickets and reporting people for summons, low-level stuff like that.

Oh, and persecuting innocent motorists obviously.

We were also expected to get to know the vicinity's streets, areas and characters. There were pictures of the most prominent criminals dotted around the station – if seen, stop and search. There were also photographs of the senior officers. You did not stop and search them. An important distinction.

Every copper remembers their first arrest. Or *only* arrest if they are on the Accelerated Promotion Scheme.

One morning I was given a piece of paper by the Sergeant. It looked important. He told me it was an arrest warrant, so my hunch proved correct. It had been issued by the local Magistrates Court because someone hadn't done as he was told. Magistrates are local worthies who enjoy telling poor people what to do. They believe that the oiks stood before them are genuinely chastised when they give them a jolly good dressing down.

For more serious matters, the Magistrates send the case to the Crown Court. Crown Courts have people who balance wigs on their heads and wear capes, despite not being super heroes.

In this instance, the subject of the warrant had been ordered to Court to face a charge of theft. Clearly not arsed, he hadn't bothered to turn up. The Magistrates waited ages and got really cross. The clerk typed-out said warrant, thereafter signed by the

Magistrate with a quill pen. In this instance, for reasons best known to himself, the subject had told the Court his real address. A lot of criminals give false ones to evade justice. 252 Uxbridge Road was very popular. Aka Shepherds Bush Police Station.

Anyway, this bloke lived just around the corner, so I ate a Mars Bar, whole, and headed round there with a fellow newbie. The door was opened by a woman smoking a cigarette, who gestured us in without speaking. A large Irishman in a white vest lay sprawled across a bed. He said he'd been expecting us, like a Bond villain. Then he asked if he could 'have a shit' before we took him away. Unlike a Bond villain. It seemed churlish to deny him that and off he went for a bit of me-time. He didn't ask for our warrant cards to be shoved under the door, but I was ready.

We got a lift back to HQ in the station van, a white Sherpa with police livery on the sides. In the back are a couple of benches that people fall off if it takes a corner too fast. As a probationer, I didn't expect verbal communication, but thanked the driver anyway when we stopped. A station's cell area is known as the Custody Suite, where permission to bring a prisoner in has to be sought from a Custody Sergeant. This is never granted straight away. Instead, you must hang around for ages while the Sergeant – inevitably grumpy – finishes his cigarette and reads *Playboy*.

You stand before him, culprit alongside, and explain why you are there, your grounds for making the arrest and why they need to be locked up. If the Sergeant agrees with your rationale, in they go. If not, the prisoner is out the front door. That doesn't happen very often or it would make the police look silly.

'Why's he not got no trousers on?' the Sergeant asked on this occasion, throwing me completely. A double-negative was the last thing I'd expected. Suddenly, I felt totally out of my depth.

'He needed to defecate, Sarge,' I replied, when in reality I had been so intent on not upsetting the driver I'd forgotten to get the prisoner dressed. The Sergeant threw me the sort of glance I would soon get used to and picked up his pen. 'What's this for?'

'It's a writing aid that dispenses ink over a ball at the end, Sarge,' I said. Well, I thought it was funny.

'The fucking arrest! What's he been fucking arrested for?' he yelled, seemingly agitated. I was ready for this bit, though. In fact, I had been practising it.

'At zero eight hundred hours I was proceeding west on Uxbridge Road, London W12, when I had cause to knock at the suspect's door. I used four of the five knuckles on my right fist,' I went on, displaying said fist and demonstrating the movement used. 'I was in possession of a warrant of arrest issued by West London Magistrates Court ordering his arrest and presentation before the Court. We were offered access to the premises by a white female with a questionable hygiene regime. I do not know her name, or date of birth, but I would recognise her again.

'I would describe the flat as dimly lit and furnished to a level expected of people who are overpaid benefits. In the flat was a bed. A large bed. On the bed was a man. A large man. A man I now know to be this man. I can confirm that the man on the bed is the same man I present before you now.

'I introduced myself as Police Constable Byrne of Shepherd's Bush Police Station and allowed him to defecate. At the conclusion, I arrested him on suspicion of failing to appear at Court. I then cautioned him, to which he made no reply at zero eight ten hours. He was then conveyed to Shepherd's Bush Police Station in a marked police vehicle, call sign Foxtrot Hotel two zero. I did not speak to the police driver at his implied insistence, but did offer my thanks at the conclusion of the journey. I did not fall off the bench. Once at Shepherd's Bush Police Station, I relayed the facts to the Custody Sergeant. Thank you very much for being here today.'

The Sergeant eyed me with disgust. 'You just had to say "It's a warrant" for fuck's sake,' he said before walking to the caged area and lighting another roll-up. I felt I had been left to carry on the booking-in process while the Sergeant calmed down a bit.

All persons arrested are subject to a search, any property listed on the Custody Record. Some were known to secrete items such as cigarette lighters in their anus. In later years, they would learn to squeeze mobile phones up there, giving a whole new meaning to 'pocket dialling'. I asked my man to put his stuff on the desk and patted him down in proscribed fashion. As he was only in vest and pants that didn't take long, but I felt it drew us closer. The Custody Sergeant then returned, telling the prisoner he could use a solicitor for free and have someone told he'd been arrested. He was also offered chance to read the Codes of Practise drawn from the Police and Criminal Evidence Act. Since the time of Sir Robert Peel, nobody has ever made use of this right. Even the police don't bother. It's all words with no cartoons, so who can blame them?

I was told to put the guy in a cell, after which the Custody Sergeant never spoke to me again, but I had made my first arrest. Feeling rather pleased with myself I then went to the canteen to make notes and enjoy a well-earned poo.

As with the eighteen weeks at Hendon, ten weeks of Street Duties seemed to go on forever, after which I was to put away childish things and become a man. A genuine *police*man. We celebrated its end by meeting for drinks in Camden. I was given the address of a pub that turned out to be a leather fetish establishment, from where I made my excuses and left. Honest.

We were now posted to one of several Emergency Response Teams covering Hammersmith and Shepherd's Bush, as part of the immediate reaction to emergency incidents and anything else other services couldn't be bothered with. Each had an Inspector, some Sergeants and a smattering of constables, amid which latter group an unofficial hierarchy existed based on length of service, skill set or seniority within the Freemasons. I was very much at the bottom of the pile. A probationer.

Each team was split in two. Half worked from Hammersmith, the rest from Shepherd's Bush, where I was posted to Team 3 to the eternal regret of those alongside me. We'd gather at either 6.00am, 2.00pm or 10.00pm before providing twenty-four hour cover as demanded by hard-working families. This was known as parading and we were expected to get our appointments out for the Sergeant when he entered the station.

Hammersmith was the Divisional HQ and had recently been rebuilt. Two police buildings were to be merged, but this required the purchase of an Italian restaurant that lay between them. The owner refused to sell, so the station was built over his eatery. And despite literally being surrounded by the Metropolitan Police, the establishment was once actually broken into: 'Officers are seeking a burglar with massive brass balls.'

Hammersmith also hosted the police's Mounted Branch, who put on legendary Christmas dos until some spoilsport Chief Superintendent decided barrels of beer, huge horses and amorous coppers on police premises weren't a good match. Yes, he actually did ban Christmas. Another probationer was told that among a Station Officer's duties was encouraging the horses to urinate. This certainly took the Mounted Branch Inspector by surprise when, on arriving for work one morning, he discovered one probationer leading them around the yard in circles while studiously examining their penises. The Chief Superintendent was told and 'did his nut', before banning practical jokes as well.

Actually, there was no chance whatsoever of that.

One day, the phone rang while I worked in the front office at Shepherd's Bush, dealing with queries and complaints from the public. It was the Sergeant pretending to be the Chief Superintendent. I duly stood to attention, saluted, and asked what I could help Sir with. He advised that complaints had been made about my protruding ears, and ordered that I glue them down.

The Sergeant's role is key in policing, involving far more than encouraging probationers to self-harm. The Sergeant is the first supervisory role. They 'support and develop Constables', when not prioritising their own promotion that is. In such cases, their priority becomes finding a bus to throw officers under, a very popular activity across all ranks of the Met, and compulsory in fact for those indulging in corruption. More of which later.

Like the first arrest, every police officer remembers their first Sergeant. Mine was an overweight Irishman.

Our Sergeant was a formidable leader. He ruled the roost and tolerated no nonsense. He had his work cut out with me in that respect. Our team Inspector spent a vast amount of his time at Hammersmith to avoid this Sergeant picking on him.

There was another Shepherd's Bush Team 3 Sergeant, though, who would go on to retire many years later as a Detective Chief Superintendent and head of the Met Police Homicide Command, a fact that never ceases to astound those who worked with the guy at Shepherd's Bush and had the pleasure of joining him for post-work refreshments in the Carlton Club.

These two Sergeants made the lives of criminals a misery. Most notably on the East Acton Estate, where the first was honoured with the graffiti: SERGUNT ***** MASTERBATS.

Area Car drivers followed Sergeants in the hierarchy. They were trained to drive really fast and allowed not to do paperwork or touch smelly people.

One area car driver was an excellent 'thief taker'. He knew every criminal in Shepherd's Bush with a sixth sense for spotting a car-ful. As his passenger, or Operator as we were called, I would be expected to get out of the car and speak with the driver first. I often had no idea why we'd stopped them, so when asked that by the driver I usually figured honesty was the best policy.

'What you stopped me for?'

'I'm afraid I've absolutely no idea. Sir.'

Another Team 3 Area car driver was a bit of a maverick. A remarkably entertaining and highly capable police officer, it was his destiny to be medically retired after injuring his knee in a fight I started in the Station Office at Shepherd's Bush. Which was not an uncommon occurrence actually.

One cold dark evening I was posted as Station Officer, which meant I had to remain within its confines. A modern equivalent might be officers placed on restricted duties due to being nonces. I was not a nonce, but I *was* a probationer and therefore a prime candidate for boring roles Masonic officers took no interest in. It involved dealing with any members of the public who walked in. Many were disgruntled drivers, often red-faced bores who felt the law should not apply to them. They would come very close to exploding with rage when a scrawny ginger haired copper who looked about twelve took their driving licence away.

A man and woman came in, the latter saying she had been assaulted by her boyfriend. I took down a few details and asked where he was. Much to my surprise, she indicated the bloke who until then had been standing silently by her side.

All hell broke loose.

The man went berserk and attacked every police officer in reach. The very devil, he was. Once he got going he refused to desist, despite one officer getting Welsh on his ass, finally ending up in back of a police van as we licked our wounds. Not literally. I'm famously unsupple. Anyway, it was during said melee that this Team 3 Area driver managed to introduce his kneecap to the corner of a table. Career over.

My favourite memory of the guy, though, is sadly unsuitable for publication. Moonwalking bicycle thieves indeed.

At some point, our first Sergeant had the honour of no longer having to line manage me. He was promoted, I think, or maybe had some dirt on the Chief Superintendent. The other Sergeant too disappeared overnight, so Team 3 gained two brand new sparkly Sergeants who we had best call Eamonn and Holmes.

I didn't use their real first names then either, in case they flushed my head down the toilet. From Northern Ireland, they took umbrage at my hilarious Ian Paisley impersonation while on parade one morning. I got sent on foot patrol, hair still dripping wet. Being a probationer, I was still in the fledgling stage of my police evolution, an amoeba in a helmet and, along with starting fights in the front office, probationers had less thrilling tasks to undertake.

Crime scenes needed guarding, which often meant being left on your own all night, proper scary. I had a morbid fear of having something dropped on my head and never being able to remove that helmet again. CID would turn up the following morning and strut around like proper throbbers before swanning off for a pint. You would at least have the thrill of writing their names in the Crime Scene Log, if you could still feel your fingers.

And then there were hospital guards. Some people who end up in police cells are not in the best of health. Some are blooming liars. Both sorts often complain to the Custody Sergeant that they are under the weather. The police doctor then gets paid a massive wedge of cash to say they need to annoy the doctors and nurses in A&E. And because they are under arrest, they can't be trusted, so a probationary police officer has to accompany them.

One such gentleman had an issue with piles. Despatched to the hospital, I was sent with him. Before long, a young doctor was hard at work pushing them back up with one finger. I did check his rubber glove wasn't flammable, in case there was a cigarette lighter up there. I really didn't want to be in that cubicle with Mr Piles but rules is rules. Throughout the procedure, he was telling the medics I'd kicked his ass grapes out during some imaginary confrontation. The doctor, a *Guardian* reader by the look of it, gave me a dirty look, only too willing to believe it. We'd never even met and, anyway, is that physically possible?

Another role for probationers was jailer. Or gaoler for any French speakers. This meant you would spend a shift being the Custody Sergeant's gofer. You'd also look after the prisoners, which mainly involved taking them into the caged area to smoke fags and try to turn them into informants.

One shift, around Christmas, two lads were brought in, accused of scrapping. Ben was tall and skinny; Bill shorter and heavy set. Bill and Ben the fighting men. It was a busy shift and they were processed fairly quickly by the Custody Sergeant, who was eager to open that day's door on his *Razzle* advent calendar.

Ben started pressing his buzzer not long after going in the cell. I sauntered down, giving it the big one. I was the jailer after all. I opened the flap in the door and saw Ben's face. He looked a little pale, but I'm no medical expert. He asked to see a doctor. I asked why, but he wasn't forthcoming, so I closed the flap in a noticeably dominant way.

Luckily the doctor, or FME as they were known (Fucking Medical Expert) was in his room counting his cash, one of those who talk posh and think it okay to patronise us lesser mortals. When I asked if he'd be able to look at one of the prisoners he did one of those snorting noises, as if a dog had started humping his leg, and asked me a question involving Latin. You might think I'd be overwhelmed by that, but not at all. I'd done six months of philosophy at Middlesex Polytechnic. Instead, I made the wanker sign behind his back as he strutted down the corridor to Ben.

'There's nothing wrong with you is there?', the doc observed through the flap in a matter of seconds, before going back to his wad. So Ben started buzzing again. I opened the flap and saw his hand waving around. It was covered in blood, which was gross. Then he gestured down to his trouser area.

It turned out that while he was scrapping with Bill, the larger man had gone to ground. And as he did so, had managed to grab hold of Ben's testicles through his pants, causing the skin to rip.

As I looked down, I saw that Ben's other hand was holding a testicle, outside the sack of skin it is supposed to be in. Bollocks, I thought, feeling faint. The FME then came trotting back and decided that Ben ought to visit the hospital after all.

What had happened was literally nuts. In those days, fighting was a popular pastime, testicle ripping more niche.

As probationers, during training it was impressed on us that fighting in public was against the law. We were instructed in techniques and methods of making bad situations worse. Role plays always had bad guys doing as they were told by officers.

I was fully taken in, thinking myself proper hard. My first physical confrontation in the job was a fight outside a pub. I grabbed hold of one fellow from behind. He bent over, threw me over his shoulders and I landed on my back in the middle of the road and was almost run over by a passing bus.

Another night I was on duty in uniform. Hammersmith Palais was due to kick out, so expectations of frayed tempers were high. An arrest on foot patrol was golden. You'd be able to have a ride in the van back to the station and then have a fag in the yard like a hardman while waiting to book your prisoner in.

A young man in glasses, of slight build, stood in the middle of the one-way system blocking a bus. Onboard revellers were calling him nasty names. The kebab shop spilled out to watch and I was going to have to get involved. I had a plan of action. I'd give him a few words of advice, in a disinterested way to ensure he knew he was only a small fish in my big barrel of crime.

I sauntered over and he punched me full in the face, knocking my helmet under a bus. It wasn't enough to knock me out, but I did lose an eyelash. We then had a prolonged wrestling match in the middle of the road until more coppers came to the rescue.

The next day he was charged with assault on police and would subsequently plead guilty in court. He was fined and ordered to pay me compensation. Some weeks later, he attended Shepherd's Bush Police Station to deliver a letter. This revealed that following his conviction he'd lost his job and his girlfriend. I was a bastard; he didn't know how I could live with myself. Taped to the bottom of the letter was 25p, I assume in compensation.

I'm still waiting for the other £4.75.

3

Driving to a Different Beat – Car Trouble and Learning Curves

'Response policing' has changed in many ways since the mid-1990s, but much remains the same. Mental health issues, though, have become a millstone around the force's neck. I simply don't remember them being as impactful.

As a measure of difference, I was once in a van with another PC, sent to take a traumatised soldier from his flat to the local mental health ward. He was in the throes of a breakdown and known to have numerous weapons around his home.

We were armed only with a quick wit and the joy of youth, hoping he 'didn't take us hostage'; a belief in immortality that would fade through the years. I'm not sure what legal power we used either. The Ways and Means Act. Probably.

The soldier had been in a combat zone. He'd been in charge when a roadside bomb had taken them out. One of only two survivors, he blamed himself for the deaths of others. A decent, honourable man, he recognised that he needed help. He knew his mental health was fractured and feared he might harm people. He wasn't worried about taking his own life.

We left his flat, chatting peacefully, knives and machetes safely locked away behind us. But as we drove off, something changed in him. He began talking in army slang. He had been transported back to the day when his comrades were murdered. He believed that he was in a war zone and that we were fellow soldiers.

He began barking orders, shouting for us to get down. He was screaming at us not to drive the way we were going. He was convinced we would be blown up. We played the part. We were part of his trauma. We made progress through traffic, convincing him that we were getting away from the danger zone.

And as we arrived at the hospital, he came back to reality. He knew what had happened and apologised. He shook our hands and wished us well. I hope he has since found peace.

The British public insists on the police being at their beck and call twenty-four hours a day. This was, to be frank, a pain in the arse and led directly to my being on duty one morning when someone tried to kill me.

I was out with a colleague in a Panda car they gave us to drive about in, looking for people to impose the will of the state upon. If we didn't find work to do ourselves the Sergeants would get Northern Irish on us and, because we were in uniform, we weren't allowed to smoke or play 'offensive music'. This would be one of the prime reasons for a move to CID in later years.

The police radio was quiet. Too quiet, I will now add with a knowing wink. Our radio channel only covered Hammersmith and Shepherd's Bush Division, controlled from Hammersmith CAD Room. This was the beating heart of the Division, according to the people who worked there and nobody else ever, populated with people who liked to tell other officers what to do at a safe distance. I was in self-imposed exile from the place having accidentally compared a civilian member of staff there to Pat Butcher out of *EastEnders*.

The faster police cars had 'main sets' which transmitted calls pan-London from Scotland Yard. The call sign of Scotland Yard was MP. No idea why. The Radio Operators all used received pronunciation, as one would expect.

Listening to the main set gave you an understanding of what was going on right across the capital.

A posse of riot police called the Commissioner's Reserve was always on duty. The TSG as they were formally known (Thick and Stupid Group to us) travelled in packs of three carriers containing an Inspector, three Sergeants and a load of Constables. If the Commissioner got into bother he could call them up. Armed 'Trojan' units were also deployed over the main set, albeit in motors not wooden horses. It made for quicker deployment but did sacrifice the element of surprise.

So anyway, as my colleague was driving us aimlessly around Shepherd's Bush I noticed he seemed on edge. Up late perhaps, I reasoned, battering some heroin dealer. We didn't have the main set to listen to, so I was whistling a happy tune when two armed response vehicles hammered past us, heading towards Acton. We waved but they ignored us, because we were probationers in a Panda and they had guns. I gave my whistle an impressed note.

Moments later, the CAD room told everyone there had been an armed incident there. A young gentleman had been minding his own business when all of a sudden three armed men had burst into his flat and demanded payment for a drugs shipment. They'd put the barrel of a gun in his mouth as well, so had clearly been watching too many American movies.

The radio described how the suspects had then made off in a red Vauxhall Astra, which turned out to be stolen. They gave a registration number that I immediately wrote down on the back of a fag packet, 'cos I was street. Then I looked up. 'Bollocks!' I said. We were right behind it. The car in front was full of men with guns. 'Bollocks!' concurred my colleague.

The armed coppers were miles away in Acton. We were on our own. Two unarmed probationers in a Panda. We had to keep an eye on them without them realising we were there, which was tricky as we were dressed up as policemen in a fully liveried police car with a blue light on top. Still, we gave it a go.

I dropped my radio handset into my lap so they wouldn't see I was transmitting. The driver kept checking us out in the rear-view mirror, though, and looked properly suspicious.

We stayed with the Astra as they carefully abided by the speed limit and stopped at pedestrian crossings. It was gratifying to observe that, despite being heavily armed gangsters, they still had respect for the Highway Code. We drove past the BBC on Wood Lane, the occupants of that famous building unaware of the drama unfolding on their doorstep.

Meanwhile, I continued shouting updates at my crotch. The Control Room Sergeant had taken over; someone had obviously thought it serious enough to disturb his morning nap. He told us not to attempt to stop the vehicle and that he'd asked for armed police to save us. 'No shit, Sherlock!' I shouted, without pressing the transmit button. I felt a spray of sweat from my partner at the wheel, could smell his fear, both of us realising that our lives were in the hands of some of the most dangerous men in London.

Soon, the Astra showed good lane discipline and indicated left onto the dual carriageway that leads up to the A40.

I saw their driver check his mirrors and told mine I was too young to die as we tailed them to the next roundabout. Turn left again and they could make off along the A40. Right, and they'd be going into town. Or they could go all the way around, of course, and head back the way we'd come. Which is exactly what they did.

And so did we. Which really gave the game away I felt.

Suddenly, the Astra pulled onto the hard shoulder without

indicating or activating hazard warning lights, so it was obvious that things had changed. We drove right up next to them, to look at the driver. At which he and his mates chose to get out and run, rather than shoot me in the face. Which was nice of them.

A wall backed onto the Edward Woods Estate, a sprawling place full of tower blocks and dark alleyways that had a notorious reputation in police circles. As do all council estates, actually. Two suspects were over it before we were out of the car. The third was of larger stock, not built for sprinting – or clambering over walls for that matter. He was struggling to get over one as we caught up and pulled him off. Suddenly he produced a knife, which he swung in an arc towards my head. My colleague blocked his thrust with an arm, but the knife still went into my hand and luckily no further. At which I decided to knee our combatant in the testicles, knowing I'd have only one shot at it. If I did it hard enough, he'd crumple. If I didn't, he'd stab me to death. Happily, he fell to the ground clutching his balls and we managed to handcuff him just as the armed coppers turned up. One of them gave me a wink. Either that or he had a nervous twitch. I hope it was the former because an armed cop with a twitch is a dangerous beast indeed. Anyway, they wrapped us in silver blankets – the ambulance service insisted, don't know why, we hadn't run a marathon – and months later I received a Commendation. It wasn't for bravery. It was for supporting the Met's 'key objective of reducing residential burglary.'

Even though I'd kneed an armed man in the groin, I wasn't about to rest on my laurels. Still a fresh-faced ginger, with six months of philosophy under my belt, I had a lot of growing up to do. I was to carry on with the probationer roles of jailer, station officer and 'horse' to the bar for Sergeants requiring a pint in the pub.

And the role of night duty station officer at Shepherd's Bush never stopped giving.

Once, two blokes came in, having a proper geezer argument. Their row got more heated, despite a copper who looked about twelve (me) asking them to leave it out. 'The Boy Byrne' another nickname I acquired. Anyway, this duo weren't for leaving it out so I arrested the loudest for Breach of the Peace, the go-to reason for arrest when you can't work out what else to do. Let's call him Mr Green, because he was a grass.

I took him through to the Custody Suite where the Custody Sergeant was as usual doing his soft-porn themed wordsearch. Unwilling to disturb him, I took my prisoner for a fag and, using my best Cockney accent, milked him for information. Much to my surprise, he started telling me about drug dealers, armed ones at that. I said that the best way to deal with those was a knee to the bollocks and he thanked me for the advice before disclosing the names of a south London crime family importing cocaine. He revealed where they were going to store it, and what firepower they had.

I asked if he would like to be known as Deep Throat. He took a long pull on his cigarette. He knew secrets. Then having written everything Mr Green had said in an Intelligence Report, the word 'GRASS' under 'Source of Information', I went home to bed.

Upon waking, I noticed loads of missed calls on my mobile. There was a message too, saying to call the Detective Sergeant in the Intelligence Unit. Mr Green's info had been red hot and the Met's Drug Squad was taking over, a unit based at Scotland Yard who worked right across London and had expense accounts with free entry to nightclubs and discounts in knocking shops. My conversation with their Drug Squad detective went like this:

– Yep?
– Hello there.
– Who's this?
– Four-Ten FH.
– What?

- Four-Ten FH. PC Byrne currently attached to Shepherd's Bush Police Station.
- Is that Paul? Less of the formalities son. You ain't in court!
- My apologies. Over and out.
- What? Listen, Paul, we've had your DCI on the blower about the source you dropped last night. We're proper interested. The boss wants the SP on your snout.

I had no idea what he was on about.
- Yes.
- Yes what?
- Okay?
- You with us Paul? Few moons since I done uniform. Job still fucked down on the shop floor?
- I don't think so.
- Paul says the job ain't fucked no more lads. Voice of the people.

He was talking to other seasoned detectives in the background, who seemed to be enjoying themselves, probably drinking whisky and snorting the cocaine they'd seized.

- Now listen, son. Your snout. The boss wants me to have a word with him. I've got a monkey on the table and a pony for afters.

I still had not the faintest idea. Were we going to the zoo?

- The guv likes reassurance. He ain't a happy man at the best of times, between you and me. You know the score, Paul. These are the big boys and this could chop their bollocks right off. If your geezer is on the money, we're looking at doing the drum with a ticket early doors. Be a dig out around the shooters. Run me through the chat.
- Yes.
- Yes, what?

– Yes, please?
– Eh?
– Sorry.
– Paul. Just tell me what the fucking geezer said to you.
– Right. So he said they'd get the brown and white and maybe some... puce? I think he said? Then they'd chop everything up while the older one uses his nostrils to smell the flowers.

He hung up on me.

I was Station Officer again the next night, when my phone rang. The caller ID showed: Mr Green the GRASS (My first informant! WHOOPEE!)

This time he said the drugs and guns weren't there. Then he said, 'I was winding you up!' and laughed. I hung up, bottom lip quivering. I'd have to tell the Drug Squad because they'd given the strong impression they were going to do Drug Squad stuff.

– Yeah?
– It's Four Ten FH. PC Byrne. Currently attached to Shepherd's Bush Police Station. Over.
– Paul?
– Yes. I didn't wake you, did I?
– What?
– I said I didn't wake you, did I?
– I heard. I'm with the guvnor. The OP has eyes on. Giving the off in next twenty. The Trojan boys are plotted up.
– The informant man called me. Just now. He says the drugs and guns aren't there.

The Drug Squad Detective Chief Inspector came on the line. It was two in the morning and he was in charge of a full-scale armed operation against a notorious south London crime family. A ginger probationer from west London was now telling him it was a wind-up. He used some really nasty, horrible words that I still feel faint thinking about. I'd been burned by a snout and not for the last time, you won't be surprised to read.

I never heard from the Drugs Squad again, disbanded a few years later. Would they still be going if my big case had gone ahead? Maybe recycling seized drugs had more to do with it.

Policing was a steep learning curve; I'd certainly picked up new and inventive ways to use the C word. A few weeks after taking my revenge on Mr Green by forcibly deleting his number from my mobile phone, I was summonsed to the Team Inspector, who yelled that I should hand over my warrant card due to some trifle about having had one too many the night before attending Crown Court. It had been alleged that I'd given evidence whilst intoxicated. You'd think barristers would have a better sense of humour given they balance horsehair wigs on their bald patches.

On top of that, pre-shift parades became more exciting. I was being posted with experienced officers who'd take my cigarettes and dinner money and sometimes twist my nipples.

The police car passenger is called the Operator. Sometimes I'd be allowed to use the main set, although the tougher drivers liked to use it themselves while driving one-handed. Some even managed to smoke at the same time, which was proper ace. When a call came in over the radio, the driver would decide whether we'd deal with it. Everyone would go to a big pub fight, or an intruder alarm at the strip bar in Glenthorne Road.

If the operator took a call without the driver's agreement, he might be punched in the throat. If no-one took it, the Sergeant would start asking everyone what they were up to. Sometimes he'd come looking. If he caught you playing on the swings when you should be reporting a burglary, life wouldn't be worth living.

I found high-speed driving pretty scary, go pale and cling to the door handle. This annoyed one Irish copper who'd whack my knuckles with his baton. Quite the feat while driving like Aryton Senna.

At the start of each shift, the Sergeant would decide who

patrolled with who. I was often used as a tool of revenge against officers who had annoyed him. Some were guaranteed specific postings. The Area Car driver, for example, would always get the fastest vehicle, unless he was over the drink-drive limit.

The Station Van would be driven by the day's angriest officer, who got to meet all the local villains and help them up when they fell off the bench seats. They'd also get to deal with having fridges dropped on the van roof while patrolling the White City Estate.

One shift, I was out having my knuckles bruised and looking forward to going to the Carlton Club after work. The barman was an ex-copper who'd been sacked for drinking and driving, so definitely not a Freemason. Pottering around Shepherd's Bush a call came out and it was time for more fast driving.

The Area Car driver decided to attend the same incident and took pleasure in overtaking us in his flashy police Ford Sierra with go-faster stripes. We were in a battered old Sherpa, so knew our place. As the Sierra disappeared towards Goldhawk Road ahead, we went through a red light. The police are allowed to do this because they'd be a bit shit as an emergency service if they didn't. We had our blue lights on, two-tone horns blasting and the driver had an angry red face, so we couldn't be missed.

By everyone except the man who'd fallen asleep at the wheel that is, and crashed at high speed into the side of our van. We juddered across the roadway, hit a raised kerb and managed to end up onto two wheels, my colleague somehow below me rather than alongside. Hanging by a seatbelt, I released a manly scream. After what felt like an age, the van then righted itself and I got out. My first inclination was to race back towards the culprit shouting, 'You stupid bastard!' Having caught up with me, my colleague, laughing hard, advised against it, suggesting instead that Rip Van Winkle be dealt with by someone less emotional, such as the Traffic Sergeant who would now be on his way.

Traffic Sergeants are a unique breed, often total arseholes. They deal with road incidents and decide whether the officers involved get to carry on or are sent to the naughty corner. Ours arrived in a little white hat and ended up giving my oppo points on his police driving licence.

It wasn't all fun and games. Police work could also be desperately sad. Upon joining the police, I assumed they could solve all the ills of the world, but that was never the case.

I remember one old lady in particular, in her eighties, stooped with age, her eyes coated with cataracts taking her vision, day by day. She lived alone, in a flat buried deep in the White City estate. Whatever family she had were gone, no friends left, living alone on the fourth floor of a tower block.

One day, she needed to go to the Post Office, behind a general store on Bloemfontein Road, next to the General Smuts pub where disputes were settled with shotguns fired into the ceiling. That was the only way to collect her state pension, a miserable collection of notes and coins to mark her declining years.

She would go out slowly, take her time on the stairs if the lifts were broken again, and cautiously pick her way between the cars that slalomed across the estate, always in the morning. The walk took time, her vision shimmering between flashes of light and darkness. She took care not to step into the road until she was sure it was clear, nor trip on anything on her way to the shops.

When the money was passed under the screen, she would be careful to put it in her purse, then her handbag. Sometimes she would buy a few groceries from the general store, but not today.

They attacked her outside the shop. She stepped onto the pavement and they attacked her. They grabbed her handbag, its strap across her body, and dragged her down the street until the strap broke. We arrived at her flat. Some good decent people had helped her home, wiped the blood from her face and made her a cup of tea. She was sorry to bother us, hadn't realised anyone had called the police.

It was the third time she had been mugged in a month.

Unwilling to go to hospital for a check-up, there was no-one familiar we could call to come around. She was sure we had better things to be doing. She couldn't tell us what her attackers looked like, what with her eyes getting worse all the time. So that was that. We'd go back to the station and put a report in. There wasn't anything to go on, so it would be filed away. Maybe the Robbery Squad would run an operation around there, maybe an informant would come forward with names, but there wasn't a great deal of hope. We'd see if we could get Social Services involved, try to get her some support, maybe a move. And then we were called back to her flat.

We pulled into the car park outside her block, from where we could see her, at the edge of her balcony, four floors up. We ran up the stairs in a hurry. Somehow, she had managed to drag a chair out, climb on it, but didn't have enough physical strength to throw herself over.

We helped her back inside, where she sat on her sofa and sobbed. An ambulance crew came, but they couldn't do much to help either. They would take her in, see whether that would spur Social Services into action, but there were no guarantees.

Sometimes, there are no happy endings.

Night Time is the Right Time – for Triumph and Tragedy

I enjoyed night shifts most – cops and crooks haunting the streets while decent people had fitful dreams. A handful of police versus the criminal world. Hear me roar!

I loved plain clothes work too, aspiring to become a detective, despite my informant hiccup. Plain clothes work on the Response team was the first step on that slippery ladder.

One night, along with another officer, I was honoured to be tasked with patrolling Shepherd's Bush in plain clothes on a pedal cycle. Our Storno radios were the size of house bricks and sat heavy in our anorak pockets. Even so, we managed to wrap the cable around us, allowing the handset to dangle in our armpits, while sporting Walkman headphones.

Having cycled around aimlessly for an hour, things had begun to chaff when the Area Car driver reported spotting three ne'er-do-wells lurking on the White City estate. He asked us to keep an eye out and we found them fairly quickly. Standing together on the estate edge, they were obviously plotting wrong-doing. We cycled past, trying to exude urbane nonchalance while sporting orange felt headphones and having conversations with our armpits. Four seconds later, we were out of sight. Carrying out observations on streetwise yobs from a moving pedal cycle at 2.00am was harder than we'd expected.

Then I had a great idea. Probably one of the key ideas of my entire policing career: I'd get off the bike and push it. Feign injury. Use my genuinely sore buttocks for a policing purpose.

I didn't have time to properly brief my colleague, who'd cycled off ahead. I acted as I'd never acted before, three criminals the audience for my debut performance. As my pedal partner exited stage right, I entered the spotlight. My mere presence on the street held them raptured. My dismount and demonstration of bottom pain was method acting at its peak. Much to my surprise, the three of them jogged over and surrounded me. An unscripted piece of improvised street theatre I certainly hadn't expected.

'That's my bike!' said one, taking hold of the handlebars.

'Give him his fucking bike back,' said another.

My mind was racing. I ran through all my Hendon training in milliseconds. I couldn't recall being trained in how to deal with getting mugged on duty.

The third one disappeared behind me, shortly before I felt a punch to the kidneys. I maintained my composure and didn't cry. I had to think on my feet before they put me on my back.

'It's not your bike,' I countered. 'It's mine.'

Another blow to my back. Then a punch to the stomach as the front one tried to pull the bike out of my grip.

'It's my bike.' I yelled. 'My mummy gave it me for Christmas.'

To this day, I have no idea why I brought my mummy into it.

Well, it all went a bit wrong after that. I ended up in a robust tussle with the trio, determined not to relinquish control of my 'present'. At one point, one of my tormentors managed to get astride the bike and tried to ride off as I hung onto the saddle. I injured my genitals on its spinning back wheel, but didn't let go. Thankfully my plain clothes partner had seen it all unfold and summoned aid on the radio in his armpit. Valuable minutes were wasted persuading the control room that, yes, his colleague was actually being mugged and, no, he wasn't taking the piss.

Eventually, the cavalry arrived and my three assailants were arrested for attempted robbery, their bewildered faces a picture. Us two, meanwhile, were told to ride to Hammersmith station and write statements. I had expected a lift after what I'd just been through; how brutal police culture can be. The night duty CID officer dropped by to see us. 'You're fucking kidding me,' he said.

'When will the CID vacancies be advertised?' I asked. My ambition could not be rocked by the cancer of street violence.

He walked away without speaking.

Next day, all three suspects were interviewed by the CID and charged with attempted robbery, a very serious offence that often carried a prison sentence on conviction. They pleaded not guilty and their case came to trial at Crown Court some months later.

I was called to give evidence before judge and jury, the events of that night burned into my brain. Under questioning, I related everything I remembered, including my claim that my mummy bought me the bike for Christmas. A female juror lost control at this point, laughing so hard the Judge had to direct the jury to withdraw and compose themselves. They came back after fifteen minutes, but the same juror burst out laughing again as soon as she looked at me. After a second withdrawal she managed to contain herself – and then they found all three not guilty.

I would never be mugged on duty again.

October 1995. I had been a policeman for just over a year. At the bottom of the pile, lowest in the pecking order, I was still in my probation period and so did what I was told. One night, I was volunteered to stay on and do four hours overtime after the team finished a late turn at 10.00pm. Another officer would work with me to carry out foot patrols around a part of Shepherd's Bush that had lately been plagued with burglaries.

Some shifts can be eye-wateringly busy, others so quiet you almost wish for something to break the monotony. The streets were silent, houses and flats in darkness as Shepherd's Bush slept. We walked side by side, up and down, round and round, as the clock ticked slowly and minutes stretched painfully into hours.

Well away from the station, it would be bad form to nip back for a cup of tea and a smoke. Our own team wasn't on nights so we felt like guests in someone else's home. The other lad had been in service a few years longer than me, so I was happy to take his lead, follow unwritten protocols. Nobody ever told you the ways of the policing world, but you soon knew about it if you crossed the invisible line. So we stayed on the beat and got on with it.

Up and down, round and round, until all we could hear was our own boots scuffing across pavements, conversation emptied, just thoughts of home and bed after a wasted night.

Between us, we agreed that one more loop would kill another twenty minutes, then we'd head back to let the Duty Sergeant know we were done for the night and seek his dismissal.

Until, walking around a corner into Askew Road, we saw a building on fire. A three-storey pile split into flats, minicab office on the ground floor. There were flames in the windows and thick black smoke gushed into the sky, darkening the street lights and circling around us. We sprinted across the road, demanding more police units and the fire brigade via the radio. Alongside the block we found a door, buzzers up its side suggesting this was an entrance to communal flats. Smoke continued to billow around us as the intense heat, feeding on the night air, pushed us back.

We began shouting, yelling through the doorway, before the smoke got into our lungs, making us cough and retch. No-one was coming out. It had just gone half past one in the morning. If people were in there, they would surely be sleeping. Through the now broken and flaking front door, we could see a flight of stairs. Somehow we got inside, covering our faces with the crooks of our elbows, our thick police jumpers offering little respite from heat and fumes. We went up, shouting that we were the police and there was a fire – anyone there should move towards our voices.

The further we climbed the more we could make out voices, and screams too, somewhere in the depths of the darkness. Then women began to stumble out of rooms into hallways consumed with fire, stumbling, reaching out in panic, choking. Overcome by smoke, they were too weak to make it downstairs alone, so between us we lifted them into our arms and carried them down the three flights to a rectangle of light that spelled safety. Five times we did that, after sitting those we'd rescued on the opposite side of the road. But we still had no idea how many more might be trapped. I went back again but the smoke was getting thicker all the time and there was the sound of glass smashing and wood crashing downwards having burst into flames. I made it to the second flight of stairs where there was a small window, only a few inches wide. Lungs burning, the intensity overwhelmed me, blackness eating me from the inside. I felt the stairs bend under my feet, heard the roar of a fire monster coming for me. Oxygen gone, my lungs stopped. I tried to breathe, but couldn't.

Even then, people overhead could be heard screaming and crying above the raging torrent. I made it to the little window and smashed it with a gloved hand, gulping manically for air.

I had to go up again. Yet couldn't – and didn't. Had to get out.

Outside, other police officers from the night shift had arrived, blocking off roads, helping those we had already carried out into ambulances. People evacuated from nearby houses stood sleepily around in nightclothes, holding their children tight.

Someone shouted and we all looked up to a window on the third floor. Two women, both in white nighties, looked down at us, pleading for help. My partner and I knew the fire brigade were only minutes away. We were shouting: 'Stay where you are, it will be okay.' Everything would be okay. Just wait a few minutes.

And then one of them seemed to stand and step back a little from the window frame, before putting her arms out at her sides and seeming to float, like an angel, backwards into the darkness.

The second one was at the window now, alone. People in the street were panicking, not knowing a fire engine was around the corner. Cries arose for her to jump, more voices joining in, and so she stepped out of the window, onto a small ledge and jumped.

She jumped.

And as she jumped she caught her ankle, and as she fell she tipped forwards, headfirst towards the road. Following which there was a crack, like a gunshot, as her skull hit the tarmac.

I grabbed some rubber gloves from another officer and ran over. Shaking so much, I struggled to get them on, but held her head, her shattered head, trying to do something, anything, to make it all better. Until the paramedics took over and she was lifted into an ambulance. The fire brigade were soon rushing into the building where they eventually found the body of the angel, several floors below. The timbers had given way.

The paramedics suspected my colleague and I were suffering from smoke inhalation, so we were rushed off to hospital as well, where I sat on a bed, in a cubicle, sucking from an oxygen mask. A doctor came in, not much older than me, and said the woman hadn't made it. He was sorry.

I got back to work a day or so later and tried to act normally. My night duty colleague was off sick and would leave the police due to the damage the smoke had done to his lungs. As a smoker, mine dealt with it better. I got referred to Operational Health, to chat with a nice lady. She thought I had PTSD, Post Traumatic Stress Disorder. I thought I hadn't the right to suffer. I was alive, wasting time, ought to be back to work, putting all this behind me. Yet I felt guilt and shame, had nightmares most nights and drowned my sorrows accordingly. I was becoming a stereotype.

Very Important People – and A Day at the Football

Policing the capital might also involve being bussed into Central London to look after those who have decided they are Very Important People. This was known as 'aid'. I was sent on aid a lot in my formative years. I suspect my team signed a petition.

We would always have to arrive hours early and sit around in big buildings named after famous old coppers, but which were often re-named when said copper was found to have been bent.

In between going out the back for a fag, we'd sit around trying to look hard and check the shoulders of other officers to see what part of London they had come from. If it was less hard than Shepherd's Bush, we'd call them wankers behind their backs then pretend we were coughing when they turned around.

The main strategic objective was always not to embarrass the Commissioner as mostly they preferred to embarrass themselves.

Then we'd be told the type of uniform we'd have to wear. The aid serial had to look identical, so members of the public found it harder to identify the individual officer who'd called them a rude word. In later years, officers got identity badges. If your name was likely to cause the public to take the piss, you got exempted. I had no sympathy, to be honest. If your surname is Pigg, what the hell possesses you to join the police?

One aid requirement saw me guarding the Prime Minister of Israel, Benjamin Netanyahu, the second most at-risk individual in the world after the President of the United States we were told. He must have been gutted. Politicians are ruthlessly competitive. Hacving recently taken out a knifeman with a knee to the gonads, I felt ready for any terrorist.

Our orders were to walk around the outside of his hotel all night in bright yellow jackets. Crazed suicide bombers are often thwarted by coming face to face with a fluorescent London bobby. The thought of a good truncheoning can cause even the most ideologically committed terrorists to renounce their cause.

My shift began with some geek giving me guff about world peace. He was from Special Branch as it turned out, whose officers read broadsheet newspapers and understand the Oxford comma. Fairly niche group in the Metropolitan Police.

I was flicking the 'V' at his departing back when a car pulled over to ask for directions. That happens a lot in central London, a right pain. The rule of thumb was to send them in the opposite direction to the one you were going in, so when they inevitably got lost it was unlikely they'd stumble across you on the way back. Only on this occasion the driver turned out to be Floella Benjamin! From *Play School* and *Play Away*! I nearly fainted. She was looking for a hotel I'd never heard of. I said it was through the square window – no, I didn't, I just made something up, then went and hid behind a postbox in case she came back.

I struggled to recover my composure after that but needed to pull myself together quickly. A very drunk chap was leaning against the hotel wall with his forehead. We've all been there, I thought. A brick outhouse in a suit came out, shook my hand and called me sir, which was nice. He then produced ID that revealed him as a member of Mossad, part of the Israeli security contingent. He had a wrinkly earpiece and was probably packing heat. I asked if he'd like to try on my pointy helmet.

Politely, he asked me to move the drunk along. I asked if they got *Play School* in Israel. He didn't flinch. I wondered if there was a trigger word that made him kill and hoped it wasn't Floella. He began to lose patience with my amiability. Either I'd move the drunk on or he would double tap him, then be spirited away as a deniable asset. I'd have to write a long statement about how some pissedhead got two bullets in the back of the head while I hid behind a letterbox. Best just to ask the drunk to move along.

'Excuse me, sir,' I said. 'Would you kindly put your penis away and proceed in a northerly direction?' He had that out now too and muttered something about police oppression.

'Sir. If you do not put your penis away and depart, you will be executed by Mossad!'

I didn't seem to be getting through to him. He splashed a drop of wee on my shoes. One last chance or I might have his brains splattered all over my trousers. I told him I'd just seen Floella Benjamin (whispering 'Floella' very quietly just in case) and all of a sudden his face lit up with shared nostalgia. We ended up hugging, before he staggered off into the darkness.

At which Mossad man disappeared like a puff of smoke.

I reasoned that up to that point he must have been the hardest person I'd ever met. Apart from Mrs Begley from Our Lady's Junior School in Wellingborough that is.

Everyone remembers where they were when Princess Diana died, don't they? Well I don't. I do remember when Trevor McDonald dropped the C bomb reading the news. Proper ace that was. And

I very much recall when Tommy Cooper died on stage, literally, and everyone laughed because they thought it was part of the act. What a way to go. Just like that!

After Di was killed, I had to go policing in Central London because the country had lost its collective mind, out in force to mourn the dead Princess. I don't remember that happening when my gran was run over by a drink driver.

I'd actually once crossed paths with Diana on an aid job back in the day. We'd all piled onto the minibus at Shepherd's Bush and begun screaming when told of our secret royal mission.

Having been driven into central London we were met by an Inspector in a sparkly uniform. Clever enough to have done a degree, we were naturally suspicious of her at first but I broke the ice by using split infinitives. A by-the-book superior type, this officer then did a formal briefing, with handouts. Uniquely, she didn't swear or use low-level violence. She told us that our mission was to protect the safety of Diana Princess of Wales, by looking out for people who could cause her harm. 'What, like the Duke of Edinburgh?' I said.

'Eh?' She replied. 'No, I'm talking about lefties.'

Being a closet *Guardian* reader I went pale, but as that was how I looked normally anyway, my reaction didn't register.

We got our orders, which boiled down to milling with tourists in Leicester Square and stopping American ones going absolutely mental when they heard Princess Di was due to turn up. At least three hours before her scheduled arrival, the place was shoulder to shoulder. Until, eventually, the Princess emerged from the Tube station and I was swept up in the scene. We all were. Here was the Princess of Hearts in a shimmering red sequin dress redolent of the splendour of ancient Queens, of Boudica and Olive from *On the Buses*. The Inspector kept her head, yelling at us to watch the crowd and look out for people with patches on their elbows, while the rest of us stared in awe at the world's most famous 'O' Level failure.

Fast forward a year or two to her death and resulting national nervous breakdown. Everything become very strange. I was sent to police the book of condolence. Also weird. People queued for seven hours to write in it. I was stationed where the line crossed a road that had to be kept clear for occasional traffic, soon a hot spot of disorder. People tried to slip silently in to save themselves two or three hours which meant others became incensed and led to pushing and shoving. Middle-aged adults fighting to write a note to a dead woman they had never met. Nowt so strange as royalists, I wish I'd thought at the time.

The London Borough of Hammersmith and Fulham has two top-flight football clubs. And QPR. Fans are keen on oppressive policing, so we often had to turn out when Saturday came.

The home of Queens Park Rangers was Loftus Road, a short walk from Shepherd's Bush Police Station, even closer if you ran. When I first became an officer, QPR *were* in the Premier League, which shows how long ago this was.

Fulham is the club for people who went to private school.

Chelsea were much bigger and had a troublesome reputation, heavily policed due to fans who loved skinhead cosplay. (I was threatened by skinheads as a boy for feeding a pony. Some things stay with you.) Their hooligan firm was called The Headhunters, in homage to a popular local chain of hairdressers.

QPR had a firm of six little lads who liked to parade around followed by police horses, so they could pretend to be hard. One Saturday, their team was hosting Manchester City. The match was rated Category B, the equivalent of a 12+ film rating, so we expected mild profanity and some nudity. In case of trouble, we went to hang out with the away fans and, ever the professional, I made sure to watch a few episodes of *Coronation Street* to brush up on the language. Such preparations weren't necessary when QPR played Manchester United, for obvious reasons.

The match was live on Sky, so we'd be under the spotlight. Man City had a large backing, the atmosphere febrile. Man City dominated and looked like taking an early lead. A powerhouse shot flew just over the QPR crossbar – and hit me in the testicles.

After crumpling on the terrace steps, I was helped to my feet by the Sergeant who called me a rude word beginning with C and I actually apologised, in a high-pitched voice, the vastly amused away fans unable to believe their luck. Bravely, I carried on, vision blurred and balance unsteady. Then City scored and they rose to their feet in celebration, one teenage boy somehow contriving to punch me in the face and send my helmet flying. It was the lad's first away game and his dad looked mortified.

The Sergeant popped over once again and wasn't sympathetic. He said to get into the crowd and get my helmet back or he would dock my wages. I suspected he didn't have the power, so quoted police regulations. As I recall, he too took a swing at me.

Come full-time, one City fan patted me on the back saying it was the best entertainment he'd had in over twenty years of following the side. I felt I had to acknowledge him, so quoted *Coronation Street*: 'Tracy Barlow! I mean, even her initials are a killer disease!' Then the Sergeant came at me so I ran back to the station and put my gonads in the fridge.

Wannabe Detectives – and other stories

By the dawn of 1998, Divisional Policing was no longer a thing. Policing would now be based on London Borough boundaries, which meant suddenly we became Hammersmith and Fulham Borough, drawing the posh officers of Fulham into the mix. They were mostly horsey types without chins, but generally okay.

I'd spent four years in uniform on an emergency response team. Learning a lot about life, my colleagues had also learned a lot about me and I had it decided for me that it was time to move on. I had my eye on the CID. Always wanted to be a detective.

The CID was basically a bunch of men in suits based at Hammersmith in order to be nearer the pubs, headed by a Detective Chief Inspector with the beard of a street fighting man. Ex-Flying Squad, he had once been on the actual telly actually saying, 'Attack! Attack! Attack!' before the Sweeney took some actual villains to the pavement. Not long after, a policy person at Scotland Yard deemed the word 'attack' overly aggressive and it was replaced with the more passive 'Go!' I felt we were just one short step away from giving up.

The DCI had heard about my fibbing informant and made a snorting sound whenever our paths crossed. That wasn't so bad. The first step to getting into the CID was getting your face known by the senior officers. Even if they did think you were a twat.

It wasn't easy getting in. It required grit, determination and bribery. I had spent my last few months on response actively gathering evidence for my application. I needed to prove to CID management that everything they'd heard about me wasn't true.

When we weren't chasing around dealing with emergency calls, we had 'spare days' when the bosses expected us to do police stuff, trying to catch baddies, while the sergeants went down the Carlton Club. I would plan and execute proactive operations. This involved working out where the crime was going on and making plans to stop it. I would arrange places for us to watch the bad guys at work, then brief officers to leap out at them yelling, 'You're fackin' nicked, my son!'

To watch bad guys at work, you'd have to be somewhere they couldn't see you. The number of criminals who commit crimes in front of police officers is vanishingly small. Unless they're punching an officer in the face outside Hammersmith Palais or trying to rob the bike his mum got him for Christmas.

We were expected to complete observations in plain clothes, to prevent our helmets from giving the game away. The police code for an observation point is OP, which stands for Ancient Place of the Watcher. Before an OP is set up, the householders sign a form saying they realise the police and criminal justice system is notoriously rubbish and that it's highly likely their details will become public knowledge, so they can get GRASS or PEDO spray-painted across their front door.

After each operation, I'd carefully add the results to my CID application and wish upon a star. And my wishes came true!

An opportunity for an attachment to the Borough Intelligence Unit was offered. Sergeant One said yes and bought champagne for the team. Sergeant Two said, 'You're never coming back. That's the best news I've ever had.' I remember those words to this day. Thanks for the support, Sarges!

I moved to the Borough Intelligence Unit (BIU), given the role of Briefing Officer and thereafter responsible for completing PowerPoint briefings for the response team.

My hope was that I'd gather more evidence to support my application to get into the CID proper.

I had to scan police intelligence reports to decide what information would be useful to response officers at the start of their shifts. Intelligence reports used to be written on paper, making them far easier to dispose of or use to blackmail informants. A new computerised system, Criminal Intelligence (SNITCH), had been brought in, much to the consternation of more old-school detectives. I was only allowed up to six items on the briefing because Scotland Yard had decided police officers were too thick to absorb more information than that. It took about ten minutes. So I got bored and started messing about.

I discovered that cartoons can be inserted into PowerPoint and entertained myself by adding wit and charm to proceedings. Knowing I'd be briefing my old uniform team, one day I cleverly created a cartoon of a gentleman doing something impolite to a donkey. I added an arrow and some text, suggesting the chap was one of our PCs nicknamed 'The Gimp', so it wasn't unfair.

I set up my presentation and chuckled smugly to myself. This was going to be a right laugh. I watched as the team filtered in and took their seats; then the Superintendent of Operations came in. I'd totally forgotten that he always did on Mondays. All faces turned to me as one of the Sergeants asked me to begin. The same Sergeant went a strange colour of purple at the antics of my cartoon creation and his donkey. I assumed the Superintendent had never seen such filth in an official Met police briefing, so just stared at the ceiling doing breathing exercises. Which was nice of him. It was all downhill from there.

Undeterred by my donkey misstep, I left my CID application on the DCI's desk with a wedge of cash in a brown envelope (or did I?) and somehow got selected for interview – the final hurdle.

My history of job interviews was patchy; I once failed one to work in an abattoir, telling them my middle name was Francis, after the patron saint of animals. Seeking work at the Inland Revenue, I suffered a reaction to my new contact lenses, so spent the entire interrogation with tears rolling down my cheeks. I bet they'd never seen such raw emotion when discussing PAYE.

For my CID interview, I asked the Borough Intelligence Unit DS for advice. He told me to make sure I'd done my flies up and wink at the panel upon introducing myself. Always worth having dirt on each of them as well, if you could. Sage advice that has stood me in good stead. He also said I should attend in full dress uniform.

On the morning of the grilling, I got there with lots of time to spare and joined my fellow candidates, who were all in regular suits. A few giggled as I sat down. Yet again, I'd fallen victim to a wind-up. At least this one didn't involve a full armed deployment by the Drug Squad.

The panel did seem a little surprised by my choice of attire as I was called in and suggested I might like to take my helmet and gloves off, while leaving my sword outside. I offered a wink to each in turn and checked my flies before sitting down.

The interview was led by a Detective Inspector who wasn't going through a bitter divorce, and had no tang of stale whisky.

He got his kicks from keeping fit and tending roses. A true maverick of the CID world. He was, though, an expert in proactive and covert policing and really put me to the test.

This DI was assisted by a senior member of Human Resources, there to advise on fairness, equality and employment law, matters that had not previously concerned the CID.

It was the dawn of politically mad correctness.

The first part of the interview was about police and CID stuff, which threw me a bit. I said I had always wanted to be a detective, and called DI Burnside from *The Bill* a great influence. Our DI just stared at me; I held his gaze but did get a bit wobbly-lipped. He then brought up my scrape with the Drug Squad informant. I think he did a bit of wee in his pants when he mentioned my getting mugged for my pedal cycle.

The HR person then took over. She asked how I would treat my victims in CID. I confidently asserted that I would provide the best service I could to each and every one of them equally. The DI started twitching and raising his eyebrows up and down. I assumed he'd had too much sugar.

This was the time of the Macpherson report, getting on twenty-five years ago now, when the Met Police were found to be institutionally racist. New legislation had been brought in, offering higher sentences for racially aggravated offences. Racial motivation was to be given due seriousness in investigations, with victims offered a far better service. This became the key thread of policing and would remain so throughout my time.

It would also be a key part of my interview for the CID. A recent pronouncement dictated that if anyone described an incident as racially motivated then it was to be treated as such. Anyone. Victims of crime would be treated in accordance with their needs. All well and good but nobody thought to inform me.

I was asked the same question again. I gave the same answer again, but louder. I assumed she hadn't heard the first time. She was properly frowning and started scribbling in about as angry a way as HR professionals can. The DI appeared to be baring his teeth and shaking his head. I'd studied body language – he must have had a really cold milkshake.

Then, and for many years afterwards, failing in the diversity section of a selection or promotion process meant you would automatically fail the whole thing. The DI was doing his best to help me out, but I just thought there was something wrong with him. I'd gone into the biggest interview of my police career ill-prepared and dressed like a Queen's footman. It wasn't going well.

The DI was giving me one last chance. He asked why I wanted to join the CID. I said, 'I want to help people less fortunate than myself (and possibly also that I cared about small animals).'

Which seemed to do the trick.

The HR professional resigned the next day.

I had made it into the CID. My journey towards becoming a real Scotland Yard detective had begun. It would be a bumpy ride.

The CID at Hammersmith was split into three departments. The regular CID was called the Main Office. Detectives refused to deal with prisoners arrested by uniform, then shredded some paper crime reports before adjourning to The Laurie Arms.

The Crime Squad dealt with robbery and burglary. Robbery is when someone nicks something but gets a bit handy with their fists. For example, if a young man is riding his pedal cycle around one evening and some ruffians set about him intending to relieve him of said cycle, that is a robbery. Even if a jury says otherwise. That then becomes a flagrant miscarriage of justice.

Residential burglary is when someone goes into a house and nicks stuff. Along with robbery, this was a key performance indicator for police bosses and figures were fiddled left, right and centre. Non-residential burglary is when someone goes into a place that isn't a house and nicks stuff. Not a key performance indicator, the bosses therefore gave not two fucks about it.

Then there was the Community Safety Unit.

The Met exists in a state of constant crisis, lurching from one disaster to the next without due care or attention. The corporate reputation of the police appears to trump all matters of humility, empathy or good old common sense. So when the Macpherson report sparked by the racist murder of Stephen Lawrence accused the Met of institutional racism, many senior officers insisted it was time for change. Only not to change themselves obviously.

Each London Borough was required to set up a Community Safety Unit. These would encompass the Domestic Violence Units already in existence, but would have wider scope.

Domestic Violence Units dealt with drunk husbands who'd been arrested having failed to take the attending officer's advice and go for a walk to clear the old head for a bit. Maybe pop in for a pint while things settled down, as if domestic violence was acceptable almost. Someone somewhere then decided that the police ought to buck their ideas up, so a 'positive action policy' came into force which usually meant making an arrest unless the attending officer had a damn good reason not to do so.

The victim was then asked to make a statement and support their attacker's prosecution through the criminal court system. Engagement in that is something I wouldn't wish on my worst enemy and I have a lot of those, so you'll understand my depth of feeling. Anyway, off to the CSU I went, and the forefront of modern policing – or so I was told.

To ensure we were all on message with the new look Met, CSU officers were sent to complete a three-week residential course at Hendon. Back to training school! I bought a new suit so I could strut around impressing the new recruits.

Hendon wasn't how I'd remembered it. The TSG weren't on standby, for one, and no sex dolls. Change for change's sake I felt.

There were about twelve of us, from all corners of the Met. I made sure not to sit near anyone from East London because they all had a rather distinctive odour and were insufferably cockney.

We were addressed by a lead trainer who decided we'd use first names. He wore Hush Puppies and kept wringing his hands as if he'd been caught naked in a Catholic confessional. This fellow told us that the police had failed the public and he accepted his own part in that. He wondered if we'd like to share our own failings, so I told him how my old French teacher used to use me as a punishment for girls who misbehaved by making me sit on their knees.

The Met had encouraged/forced some members of various communities to come talk to us about their experiences. We had a man from Brixton who had been treated badly by the police after he trying to leave the scene of a shooting. One member of the class took umbrage and asked him what the hell he'd expected to happen. This same bloke was then taken to one side by our soft-shoe lead trainer and had to say sorry.

Then some ladies from Southall complained about the police response to domestic violence in marginalised communities, and a man in a sheet talked about Druidry. One fellow from the Home Office confessed to sex in public toilets and bemoaned how intrusive he found the police. The lad who'd had to apologise to our visitor from Brixton then went a bit nuts at that point and his parents were called in to take him home.

Having gallantly put up with this, I became a fully qualified CSU officer and returned to Hammersmith ready to impose myself.

A book I read many times over before joining the police was *Talking Blues* by Roger Graaf. In it, Graaf identifies two types of police corruption. Bent for self, and bent for job. The first related to corrupt acts to enrich those officers concerned. The second meant corrupt acts intended to achieve an objective. So, fitting people up basically.

I can't recall any incidences of people being fitted up during my career. Maybe it did go on, but I'm sure it's not as widespread as some think. Fiddling of figures, though, is rampant. This may also fall into the bent for self bracket, of which I did see a lot.

The first time I encountered that was in Hammersmith CSU. A uniformed officer had found himself in a world of hurt after failing a breathalyser test. At work. While driving a police car. His somewhat novel defence was that he had been out the night before and knew he'd had a few too many jars, so his wife drove him to work. The car was then left for him, in the belief that after a shift at work he would be fit and able to drive home.

He was driving a police car because the Sergeant had given him a lawful order to do so. Whether our man told him he may be mildly intoxicated on parade or not, I do not know. I would imagine that might have turned a few heads.

The probationer he was at the time driving around with had thought it best to inform the team Inspector that his driver was drunk. Fair enough. The Inspector breathalysed the driver and due process was followed. A career hung in the balance.

The case developed and somehow the lawful order business became central. It looked like the whole case may be dropped. Until a detective provided evidence that he had seen the officer concerned driving his own car to work that morning. He was therefore now in the frame, the story concocted with his wife false. That had happened before work too, so the lawful order issue was no longer relevant.

Soon afterwards, the detective who had given evidence in a suspected drink-drive case and spilled the beans was posted to Hammersmith CSU and, a few days later, followed into a pub toilet and punched in the face by a fellow officer.

What still amazes me is that this divided opinion around the station. Some actually felt it acceptable to beat another officer up for giving evidence. I'm far less amazed now than I was then.

The whole case then collapsed amid a murk of corruption.

You Don't Have to be Mad to Smash Things Up

As part of my CID development, I was officially made a Trainee Detective or T/DC. This often upset victims of crime, unhappy about being given a trainee. I'd joke that they should imagine what it's like to line manage me, but it didn't go down well.

T/DCs were rotated around the offices to gain experience in dealing with different kinds of crime and ways of punching colleagues in the face. My next stop was CID Main Office, where I would get to wear a suit and tie. Except on weekends when we wore Trevor Francis tracksuits from a mush in Shepherd's Bush.

Our role was mainly refusing to deal with cases the uniform brought us. I was still a Trainee Detective, but in my mind, I'd found my people. Drinking whisky from a bottle in the bottom drawer and calling people 'son'? I was well up for that.

The Main Office was split into teams of detectives, each led by a Detective Sergeant. One was a Northern Ireland chap with strong convictions about religion. He was one of those characters often called 'Marmite'. A gloopy mess who lived in a jar. I told him my name was Joseph Stalin, so my real name didn't give away my Catholic upbringing.

One day, a fellow detective was directed to go out in the rain. It was to do some detective work – he hadn't been naughty or anything. He didn't have a jacket, as that can often be seen as a sign of weakness. The DS kindly offered to lend him a raincoat to protect his Crimplene suit and a trilby for his mullet. The detective put the coat on and plunged his hands into the pockets, producing a packet of white powder. Awkward. The detective was holding a bag of drugs he'd just found in his line manager's pocket. Everyone else pretended to be doing their shoelaces.

It was particularly difficult to ignore the Northern Irish Detective Sergeant who had just gone into orbit. He stormed into the Detective Inspectors'office, luckily catching them as they all tried to leg it out the building, and demanded justice.

The powder, when sent to the lab for examination, turned out to be sherbet dip. Was this a clever wind-up or a genuine attempt to fit up the DS? Who knows. I always checked my pockets after that. Better to be safe than sorry. One time I found a police warrant card with my picture on it.

Another fond memory of the Main Office is the Detective who wanted to be medically retired on the grounds of mental health. Let's call him 'Ken from *Coronation Street*'.

The trouble with Ken from *Coronation Street*'s grand plan was that he didn't have a mental health illness. Which didn't help. To be medically retired meant the top doctor people at Scotland Yard would have to agree that, due to his condition, he could no longer function as a police person and was unlikely to recover. He would be sent out to pasture with a full police pension.

If he'd been shot, or had his legs mangled in a combine harvester, brand new or otherwise, he'd have had a good case. He had a low tolerance for pain, though, which didn't help. He chose instead the invisible illness.

By coincidence, the onset of his illness came at exactly the same time as his acquisition of a West Country caravan park. He would rather be a creepy man lurking on a sit-on mower than continue as a Scotland Yard detective.

The Main Office had a row of desks holding computers, back when they were just introduced and particularly unpopular with older detectives. One day, we were all dolefully typing away when Ken from *Coronation Street*, alongside us, sent an obscene email to the Commissioner, 'part of his condition'. Then the Detective Inspector walked in. A rare treat as senior officers usually only came into the Main Office when they wanted checks done on an ex-wife's new bloke or were pissed, needing somewhere to kip. Ken saw his chance and seized it with both hands. He pushed back his chair, climbed onto the desk and proceeded to kick his computer to pieces. Then he did the same to the next one. And the next. The rest of us pretended we hadn't noticed and carried on with our work, a little disconcerting when your monitor is hoofed across the room. The DI did a backwards shuffle out of the door and was never seen in the Main Office again.

But Ken from *Coronation Street* hadn't finished. Not by a long chalk. A DS was found, who took him into the yard for a nice chat over a cigarette. They ended up fighting and had to be separated by some passing uniformed officers. Not a traditional one-to-one development meeting.

Eventually, Ken was medically retired after finding some dirt on the Chief Medical Officer. He made a great success of his caravan park where I've heard he enjoys watching people shower through a hole in the wall. He still resists computerisation mind; all bookings have to be made over the phone.

And, yes, I did fall for the famous CID practical joke of phoning the CID at Heathrow Airport and asking for DC Ten.

Following the destruction of the Main Office computers, I was moved to the Crime Squad. This meant I was now in proper plain clothes, snug jeans and boob enhancing T-shirts. The suits were put away and only dusted down for Court appearances.

As either witness or defendant.

As stated earlier, Crime Squad business was robberies and burglaries. Our outcomes would allow senior officers to be promoted, so it was all rather sensitive. If someone was arrested for either offence, we would be expected to charge them with everything we had. I wouldn't fiddle figures or concoct evidence, so was setting myself up as an outlier early in my CID career. I dread to think what would have happened if they found out I'd studied philosophy and read *The Guardian*.

There was a real stone bonker ex-Flying Squad detective who lurked in the office. He smoked indoors, and the management said nothing about it in case he still had a gun. He would regale his enraptured audience with tales from the old days, the like of which we shall never, thankfully, see again. They mostly revolved around him getting his gun stuck in letterboxes as I remember.

The Q Cars were run from within the Robbery Squad. These were unmarked police cars with stick-on blue lights. Every single criminal in the London Borough of Hammersmith and Fulham knew these cars and would shout, 'You CID innit?' as we drove past. I was secretly thrilled, but had to pretend I was all surly like the others. One car's stick-on light didn't stick on, so if we were driving fast like on *The Sweeney*, someone would lean out the window and hold it on the roof, challenging with a fag on the go.

I was in the Q Car one day when an incident took place that has become the stuff of folklore in west London policing circles. QPR won a match. I'm here all week.

Once upon a time, there was a man who lived in Shepherd's Bush, a most active gang member. Let's call this one Barry the Destroyer of Worlds. (Not his real name.)

I had dealings with Barry during my probation, when I caught him riding a moped without a properly displayed L plate. I told him he'd be reported for the question to be considered whether he would be subject to prosecution or something like that. I think he called me a twat, so was subject to a Section 5 Public Order warning. This meant that if he used sweary words again he would be arrested. It had to be fairly soon afterwards. He wasn't prohibited from cussing for the rest of his life.

Barry, alas, did not learn his lesson. It's fair to say that most of the people I admonished in the police ignored me completely, so he wasn't unique in that.

Eventually, Barry the Destroyer of Worlds got over his run-in with PC Byrne and went on to become an armed gunman. I don't imagine this was directly related, but you never can tell. The armed gunman community are a fickle bunch, quick to take offence. This was in the days before social media too, so rather than organise a Twitter pile-on, they shot one another.

Barry proved himself most unpopular and spent most of his time hiding in his mother's loft. This proved a decent idea, as the many armed chaps who came a-callin' didn't go up the loft ladder. I expect it's difficult to navigate a climb safely while doing that hard man walk, dragging one leg behind you and doing symbols with your fingers. So they battered his mum instead.

One day, Barry ventured out and found himself in Shepherd's Bush Nandos. This is a popular chicken restaurant, for those of you from Fulham. Word of his presence soon spread.

An opposing gangsta was dispatched to deal with Barry the Destroyer of Worlds. With a shooter. We shall call this gangsta Benny from *Crossroads*. (Also not his real name.) Benny turned up at Nandos and parked his Mini Metro outside. On double yellow lines. They really didn't give a damn about authority.

As Benny arrived, Barry was standing at the counter ordering the hottest food possible. No salad, bitch. Benny produced a gun, pointed it at Barry and pulled the trigger. Then he pulled it again. And again. Nothing happened.

So Barry then turned around and produced his own firearm. Like that '*This* is a knife' scene in *Crocodile Dundee*.

And *he* shot Benny.

Some grass called the police. The uniformed response was on its way. Armed officers were tucked up trying to get off with tourists in Covent Garden, so we in the Crime Squad office opted to get the Q Cars involved. I threw my coffee up the wall, stuck a fag in my mouth and leapt across the bonnet like in *Starsky and Hutch*. I'd always wanted to do that. Starsky and Hutch didn't get nose bleeds after crashing off the other side and landing on their faces, though.

Benny, shot, staggered out to his vehicle and fled the scene. Offering no quarter to the Highway Code, the bleeding gunman screeched out into traffic and struck a passing moped rider, who ended up losing a leg as a result and turned out to be his cousin. The Metro then screeched out of control and crashed through an estate agent's window where the occupant of the nearest desk had only moments before adjourned to the rear of the store to make a cup of tea. Returning with a steaming brew, he found a rapidly expiring armed gangbanger sprawled in his work station.

Let's call this estate agent Mr Fucking Lucky (his real name), who was soon joined by other members of Benny's crew who rushed to provide urgent first aid and console their friend. Oh, no they didn't! They relieved him of his gun and left him to die.

The armed police arrived and ran around in shades, while the unarmed response officers waited around the corner rolling their eyes. Once the armed guys decided it was safe, the unarmed guys came forward and stuck police tape everywhere, after which all the probationers were left to write it all up.

We turned up in the Q car and gave it the Billy Big Bollocks, having a big old debrief afterwards at Shepherd's Bush Police Station. It was difficult to establish which unit would take on the case. Local CID? Flying Squad? Murder Squad? Or Traffic for a laugh? Nobody could agree, so the DCI was called over.

He saw the nose-bleed blood on my Genesis T-shirt and asked if someone had tried to rob my bike again.

Barry the Destroyer of Worlds, meanwhile, ended up inside. He came out of prison some years later and was shot dead. I tried to get odds on that happening at William Hill but they called me a sick bastard. The best result was that Shepherd's Bush Nando's decided to offer massive discounts to coppers, just down the road from The Carlton Club. So it was a win-win all around.

A New Millennium and the Rasta of Earlsfield

After the Crime Squad, I became a fully qualified Detective. It's that easy.

We went to celebrate with a few lager tops down at The George on Hammersmith Broadway. Our achievement coincided with the *London Evening Standard* splashing news of the arrest of some former colleagues of ours on suspicion of aggravated burglary across their front page. I assumed those two wouldn't be joining us for a pint. Or their surveillance team.

The following morning, I woke with a sore head and new job. The DCI had formed an elite proactive unit and I was chosen to take part. *Cough*. We were to target the most prolific offenders in Hammersmith and Fulham, using all means necessary to bring them down. Anything to make their lives uncomfortable. I suggested sewing up the fronts of their boxer shorts.

We were given an office on the ground floor at Hammersmith station, which meant I didn't have to go down a flight of stairs to have a fag anymore. The toilets were nice and spacious as well, so I had somewhere to sleep when it all got a bit much.

The new squad was codenamed Operation Pacman. Seriously. It stood for ProActive Crime Men and Nonces, I think. We had free rein to work whatever hours the job demanded to bring offenders to justice. We worked hard, played hard and acted hard.

A key part of policing is prevention – catching bad guys in the act. It's called 'taking them over the pavement' in the Flying Squad and 'taking them for a picnic' in Community Policing.

We also got basic training in surveillance. It's remarkable how difficult day to day activities become when you're pretending not to be a policeman. The simple act of walking down a street without drawing attention becomes a fiendish challenge. You find your arms windmilling, or start skipping without realising.

Sometimes you have to get off the street by ducking into a shop and if you slip into a massage parlour, for example, you might cause lots of half-dressed local politicians to run out the back. This will definitely draw attention.

We ran an operation against a man I'll call Umpah Lumpah Stick it up your Jumper (not his real name). Umpah, a convicted paedophile, had been asked to leave Northern Ireland by some concerned citizens with ArmaLite rifles and balaclavas. He came to London under an assumed name and did a lot of wandering the streets of Hammersmith. We were to monitor his movements and try to identify any criminal offences he might indulge in.

Our basic training wasn't quite enough to fool someone who suspected they might be tracked down and executed by the IRA. He soon spotted us hiding behind bushes and talking into our armpits. Umpah got so upset he kept calling 999 to complain about Republican terrorists following him. The operators worked out he was a nonce and told him to fuck off.

The day was a great success. Umpah spent most of his time

in a state of panic but wasn't killed by terrorists. He didn't do any noncing either. The only downside was our Detective Sergeant bcame overcome with heat stroke due to wearing a thick sweater his nan had knitted for him on one of the hottest days of the year.

Operation Pacman was technically advanced. We were well versed in the latest crime-fighting techniques. We'd get a map of the area with dots on it to show where crimes had taken place. A lot of dots together was called a 'hotspot'. Clever, eh?

One day, someone noticed that a lot of cars were being broken into in a sidestreet near the A4. This was called theft from motor vehicle, a key performance indicator, and the greatest minds in the carpeted world of the Senior Leadership Team could find no way of manipulating their way out of it. So they called Pacman.

'In 2001, a crack police unit were stopped from going to the pub for crimes they hadn't solved. Made to stay on duty, they promptly escaped from a minimal security CID room to The George. Today, still wanted by the Senior Leadership Team, they survive as trainee detectives of fortune. If you have a problem, if no one else can help, and if you can find them... maybe you can hire Operation Pacman.'

So we got busy. A police car parked in the target street, and a dummy laptop computer was left in plain sight on the front passenger side. A honey trap set by the bizzies. No self-respecting thief would be able to walk past that.

Then we reviewed our approach. Someone pointed out that a fully liveried police car with blue lights on top might not appeal to our suspects, so we swapped it for an unmarked car.

Dynamic decision making in action.

The dummy laptop, when opened, read: 'Property of the Metropolitan Police Service. You're nicked!' We didn't have the budget to make it explode.

An officer armed with a video camera kept observations on

the car from a nearby window. They stayed in communication with the rest of us via police radio. I formed part of the arrest team, which didn't inspire confidence in anyone.

As a competitive bunch, we judged our masculinity on our number of arrests. At the time, my manhood was drooping, so I was determined to make one. We were on standby in the beer garden of a nearby pub, which was nice, wearing standard police plain clothes. Boots, jeans and big coats to cover our radio and handcuffs. We all wore earpieces too. These had evolved since the days of orange felt Walkman headphones, but were still quite bulky. In the height of summer, we looked like a band of lunatics, drinking halves of shandy.

Our operation commenced and it didn't take long for some well-known vehicle crime suspects to turn up. Our woman in the observation point kept up a calm and measured commentary, so we knew what was happening, fast-time. Other pub users would have seen us all getting a little over-excited as the voices in our ears told us we were close to deployment. People began quietly to move away. And then it happened. The shout came to 'ATTACK ATTACK ATTACK!' The words we'd been waiting for.

I couldn't believe the level of aggression surging through me with the unauthorised use of the 'a' word. I threw my shandy up the wall, shoved a fag in my mouth and legged it out the pub. The radio told us that one of the suspects had smashed a side window of the car and was leaning through to take the laptop. That was the last thing he did before finding me mounting him from behind. I managed to pull him off and then rode him hard as he lay, spread-eagled, on the tarmac.

The two other suspects legged it, one quickly detained. The other ran across the A4. Yes. He ran across six lanes of fast-moving traffic to avoid being nicked. It would have been far more sensible for him to take the subway, but each to their own.

And he made it. All the way across unscathed. Then he got nicked by the officers waiting for him on the other side. Bummer.

For him getting arrested, that is. It wasn't a bummer that he hadn't been killed. I'm not a monster.

I managed to force my suspect into handcuffs as he squirmed under my manliness. I then looked up and realised we were surrounded by a group of parents with buggies, who had just collected their children from nursery. And then, as one, they all began to applaud and the tears poured down my face

The turn of the millennium was approaching. I wasn't going to party like it was 1999, because all police leave was cancelled. The year 2000 would see the Met face extraordinary demands. Some senior officers believed it was the end of the world, so couldn't be arsed helping out with the planning. Times were tense.

The Met seems to be taken by surprise by New Year's Eve every single December. Notting Hill Carnival comes as a shock too and, for God's sake, nobody mention the Commissioner's birthday! They deny the existence of Christmas 'coz they is woke.

Every New Year's Eve, thousands travel to central London to stand in a large group of people without alcohol. Then Big Ben rings out at midnight and everyone looks at each other and says, 'Is that it? That's shit,' before trying to get off with one another.

I always hated going out that night because it encouraged the worst people. The sort who describe themselves as 'crazy' or 'wacky' and carry whoopee cushions and inflatable mallets, on the off-chance. When I first joined the police, I got the chance to arrest them for asking if I was a strippergram and then ruined their lives by giving them a criminal record.

But 1999 saw even the most important detectives, like me, forced into action. We would not be expected to don our old uniforms because we were all too fat due to lunching on lager in the Laurie Arms most days. We would be used in an intelligence gathering capacity. I was to form part of an Oracle unit.

Despite the name, I knew nothing.

It turned out that a few of us were to lodge ourselves on the roof of a secret location and watch people in Trafalgar Square through binoculars. This secret location was the South African Embassy. The last time I inadvertently gave away the location of an observation point, residents were harassed by local yobs and forced to move. I can't imagine the National Gallery defecating through the South Africans' letterbox after they read this book, though. I've tried to get odds on it at William Hill, but they may have taken out a restraining order.

Despite being elite detectives, we had to use public transport from Hammersmith. The Tube was rammed, so we had to sit on each others' knees. At the Embassy, we were welcomed by the Ambassador, and a flunky offered us a tray of champagne flutes. I suspected they confused us for someone else. The Canadian Ambassador and his entourage were sent up onto the roof via the tradesman's entrance and told not to look anyone in the eye, so my suspicions were confirmed.

To avoid an international incident, we felt it prudent to have a glass, and enjoy a handful of canapés. As CID officers, we were well accustomed to drinking on duty. We finally managed to have a word with one of the butlers to point out the mix-up. He looked a bit pale and went off to tell the Ambassador they were at war with Canada while we went up to the roof for a quick power nap to dull the alcohol.

Our task was to eyeball the crowd and report back. For major events, Scotland Yard controls the radios. They call themselves GT as opposed to MP, even though we all knew they were the same people. Every now and then, we'd get called up and asked for a situation report or 'sitrep' as per policing terminology. 'It's heaving. What the fuck do you expect? The Hanging Gardens of Babylon? Herds of wildebeest sweeping majestically across the plain? Over and out.' GT did not appear to recognise *Fawlty Towers* quotes, further confirming my assertion that the police service is stuffed with humourless bores.

They demanded numbers, and I went cross-eyed counting. After about half an hour, they clarified it was an estimate, not a specific figure they were after. I felt they were exacting revenge for my witty asides.

Stories had been spread that it might be the end of the world because computers couldn't cope with the change in digital dates, and might get really odd like Hal, in *2001: A Space Odyssey*. Then, half an hour before midnight, all our radios and mobile phones stopped working. I thought about forming a death cult, but didn't have time for brainwashing. My colleagues believed the Met were a benign force for good, so deprogramming through intensive psychotherapy and confrontation would have taken far too long.

Anyway, the world didn't end at midnight, did it? Instead, everyone said, 'Is that it? That's shit,' and tried to get off with each other in a futuristic way. Told to get the fuck out by the South African ambassador, we made our way back to the Tube and saw Hammersmith uniformed officers in hand to hand combat with revellers. How refreshing that people should celebrate the world not coming to an end by fighting with coppers. Everything was getting back to normal. I did some shadow boxing at the officers until a sergeant told me to piss off. And this I duly did, to the Laurie Arms, which was open all night in our honour.

I passed the Sergeants exam at Hammersmith, but slipped up on the second part involving role play. I had long since mastered the art of not shoving my warrant card under doors in the shitter by now, but anything beyond that was outside my comfort zone.

Police acting is called OSPRE 2. The Met dropped OSPRE 2 when it was pointed out that acting is a bit fey for an organisation priding itself on violent misogynism. More caring police forces still use the system, which can be seen in their use of Stanislavski techniques on mutual aid.

The acting exam involved you sitting in a room pretending

to be a recently promoted Sergeant. You'd then entertain a series of role players who would pretend to be disgruntled members of the public you couldn't arrest. The examiner sat behind you with a clipboard doing little pop farts.

I failed on diversity. If you failed diversity, you failed the entire process, regardless of how well you had done otherwise. I failed because I referred to the pretend senior officers as 'he' instead of 'they', clearly exposing my misogynistic subconscious impulses. I received the result in the CID Main Office. 'Bloody women!' I howled into the abyss. The abyss looked into me and suggested I might try to confront my own prejudices before lashing out.

I paid for a course, where a serving Superintendent instructed us on the ancient art of passing promotion processes. He was well paid for this insight, but it was okay because he'd registered it as a business interest. This meant that if you intended to carry on secondary employment as a serving police officer, you had to get authority from really senior officers. You can't use your position as a police officer to make a profit. So instructing other officers on how to pass police promotion exams was okay, apparently. I didn't get the chance to ask if he was 'on the square'.

The course was worth it though. I met two Special Branch officers who kept pretending they weren't Special Branch officers. I broke their 'bus drivers' cover story by asking the price of a single fare from Charing Cross Road to their mum's bedroom.

All of this meant I had to travel elsewhere to get another crack at the acting part of the promotion process. I stayed overnight in a hotel and was most put off by lovemaking in the next room. I wished I had headphones, but they were broken in the mugging at Shepherd's Bush, so I wrapped my head in unused toilet roll.

In the end, I remembered not to refer to senior male officers as men and did a lot of talking about the little ladies. I managed to pass. The Met Police wouldn't know what had hit it.

Luckily for them, though, I decided to defer my promotion. I had grand ideas. I was leaving Hammersmith.

One last heart-warming tale, though, before we take our leave of Hammersmith and dear old Shepherd's Bush.

Sometimes, we did pro-active stuff in the CID world. Rather than wait for the uniform to bring us work to refuse, we'd have to go out and earn our own onions. Or something. One story sticks with me because of what happened years later.

Search warrants are issued by Magistrates when they're not busy waggling their fingers at single mothers. When a copper wants to smash their way into someone's house, they need a search warrant. To obtain one, they get all dressed up, go down to the Magistrate's Court and show all the paperwork to the Duty Clerk. Invariably the level of literacy is so low they are helped to write it all out again without getting angry or upset.

The copper then gets to sit in the back of the court while the Magistrate tells off people who consider them twats. Then the copper gets in the witness box and holds a Bible in the air, before doing some swearing of his or her own.

The Magistrate will read the paperwork, then look over his half-moon specs at the copper to make sure there is no smirking or fingers crossed. If satisfied, the Magistrate signs the warrant with his quill pen. After which, the copper goes off and smashes someone's back door in.

Once upon a time my colleagues and I executed a search warrant at a barber's shop. The information was that there was loads of drugs there, which turned out to be correct. I was surprised because I thought the bloke was winding me up. I still had trust issues after Mr Green nearly got me beaten up.

There were a few people in the barber's, so I waved the drugs in the air and asked who they belonged to, telling them to put their hand up. The man in charge did, so we let everyone else go. Mainly because they were halfway through having a haircut, so looked proper daft.

The young Rastafarian man in charge of the barber's shop was arrested and subsequently charged with drug supply offences. Scrupulously polite and genteel, he was also extremely good looking. You may have noticed that I have not commented on the physical appearances of those I have described previously, apart from the fat Irishman in his vest and pants. There is a reason for doing so during this tale, as you will discover.

The case came to trial at Crown Court. I had to read out the interview transcript. The prosecuting barrister would play the part of the accused and I pretended to be me. Therefore, the jury got to listen to me asking my own questions while our handsome Rasta was played by an upper-class white man in a horsehair wig.

Thankfully, nobody mentioned the bike my mummy got me, so the jury stayed composed. Then the accused gave his evidence, the jury fell in love with him and he was found not guilty.

Over twenty years later I was walking through Earlsfield in South London, a long way from Shepherd's Bush. I was wearing full denim and had just had a feathercut, a treat to myself. I heard someone shout, 'Officer! Officer!' which often meant a need for police assistance, so threw my coffee up the wall, chucked a fag in my gob and got ready to leg it in the opposite direction.

Who should it be but the good-looking Rasta from twenty years earlier. He had recognised me after all this time and I remembered him. We spoke for a while and he complimented me on how decently I had treated him and how I'd changed his opinion about the police. I was touched by that. I'd always made the effort to treat people decently, and hadn't always succeeded.

He'd shown me why it was worth it.

Dead People Everywhere and a Night on the Toon

I felt I'd achieved everything I'd set out to do in Hammersmith CID. Nothing. It was time for a change and the Murder Squad were advertising. I went to ask my Detective Chief Inspector for permission to apply. 'Give me the fucking application and I'll write it myself,' he said. He lived with his mother and had a broken fridge in his overgrown front garden. You know the type.

Asked why I wanted to join on the application form, I wrote: 'I want to help dead people less fortunate than myself. You slags.'

I was invited for an interview and it was really grim. They just kept going on and on about death. When asked how I dealt with confrontation and disagreement, I told them I'd once stopped a Mossad agent executing someone for having a piss. I kept Floella out of it though. This wasn't her fight.

Anyway, I passed selection, became an overnight seasoned Murder Squad Detective, and hadn't had to bribe anyone. Maybe the DCI had lobbed the Squad boys a few quid.

I was now part of Specialist Operations, covering South London, and looking forward to chasing hairy-chested men in Cuban heels through deserted factories, like on the telly.

The reality was that even though we were Scotland Yard Detectives, we weren't allowed anywhere near Scotland Yard. My team was based in gentile Earlsfield, where I'd have my haircut mocked by the Rasta lad years later. We were led by a Detective Chief Inspector Senior Investigating Officer. The lead officer in any murder enquiry goes by the abbreviation DISCO BISCUIT. If you ever hear that said at a crime scene, there's been a murder; it's not a request for hallucinogenic drugs. Well, not always.

We had three bosses, the main man and a couple of Detective Inspectors. One was an envoy of the devil. Any 'bantz' and he'd say, 'Paul. A man is dead,' time would stand still and everything would suddenly become really cold. The other DI was a massive Freemason and, below them, we had Detective Sergeants too. One was Welsh and as angry as you'd imagine. And there was a cockney one who liked to earn overtime by sleeping off hangovers in police cars.

The Detective Constables were split in two. One group was diligent and professional and refused to drink on duty. They were known as 'The Quakers'. One member of that group's claim to fame was that he had once been in a phone box having a difficult conversation with his fourth wife when someone got stabbed to death up against the window. An outstanding way to end a tricky chat. And he booked on for overtime as well. Chapeau!

I was in the group that liked drink and overtime.

There were quite a few characters on the Murder Squad. One got kicked off the team following a not guilty finding at a murder trial at the Old Bailey. He'd seen fit to say, 'Not a problem. She fucking deserved it, didn't she?' within hearing of the grieving family. He claimed mental health issues and got moved to the Paedophile Squad, surely a human resources first.

I'd always had an interest in police interviews. The psychology ... battle of wits ... crossing swords with solicitors ... endless games of chance. Lead interviewers on a murder team were the cream of the crop, who'd risen to the top. Crucial evidence could be gained by cunning manoeuvres.

A murder interview is like a game of chess, as I found out one day when I was given the chance to assist in one.

I spent some time combing through the paperwork, trying to work out what angle the lead officer was going to take. I knew his years of experience would shine and expected a photographic memory and forensic grasp of detail. In fact, he said he was going for a quick lie-down; a lunchtime pint hadn't agreed with him.

An hour or two later as we prepared to go in, he suggested I start the interview by reading all the admin stuff out. I went into the interview room and shook hands with the suspect and his Solicitor, much to their surprise and poured the tea, offering a plate of biscuits around. Wholemeal. The suspect looked the type to call McDonald's a restaurant, so I felt it necessary.

I then did the preamble about having a solicitor present and informed them that throughout the interview I swore to tell the truth, the whole truth and nothing but the truth, so help me God, even though I was a Pagan. The solicitor stopped writing and just stared at me. The final thing you do before getting into the questions is read the suspect the caution. This is a very complex process that goes on for ages. As I explained it at some length everyone was glazing over, so my more experienced colleague wrote a note and pushed it across to me: 'Shut up, you prick.'

The interview was ready to begin. I was on the edge of my seat with anticipation, thrilled to witness a masterclass.

What that actually entailed was our man banging the desk a

few times while shouting, 'You did it, didn't you? Yes, you fucking did!' The suspect, meanwhile, kept saying 'no comment', until his questioner yelled that he'd had enough and stormed off for a piss. In fact, he retired soon afterwards. Last I heard he was driving a London black cab and calling up talk radio show hosts to shout about immigration.

Although mainly based in London, there was the odd occasion when we went further afield. Once, I was sent to Newcastle.

A man who'd taken a pharmacy load of drugs topped off with a Wetherspoons of alcohol decided he wanted a fight. This was in Croydon, where fighting is a popular pastime among young dandies. This bloke went up to a brick outhouse and said, 'Come on, then!' This chap then dutifully punched him to the ground. Unfortunately, he hit his head on a kerb and died, as witnessed by two brand new officers, out on patrol for the first time. One of them was sick. The Met Police Murder Squad was deployed.

Our suspect was described as a stocky white male with a shaved head going by the name Big Geordie. Our only other lead was his phone number. We decided to give it a ring and give him the chance to hand himself in. I got the job, given my lovely phone voice. 'Hello, is that Mr Big Geordie?' I said.

'What?' he replied.

'Mr Big Geordie?'

'Who's this, like?' he ventured, in a Newcastle accent.

'Oh, hello there. My name is Paul. How are you today? Great. I'm a detective Constable with the Metropolitan Police Murder Squad. Now, it's nothing to worry about, at all, but it looks like you've killed someone. We need to talk to you about that.'

He hung up. But not before we managed to trace his phone.

I went to our DCI. He asked if we'd met, as I seemed familiar. I told him I was a detective on his Murder Squad and that we were investigating a murder in Croydon, which completely threw him. He asked if one of the DIs knew about this and the room went cold. He asked for facts, but I shared my emotions. It's in my DNA. He agreed that Mr Big Geordie was a suspect and said we should arrest him. That's why he got paid the big bucks. I was selected to find a stocky white man with a bald head up north.

We flew on EasyJet because we were Murder Squad detectives and it really impressed the Cabin Crew. 'I think you've had enough to drink, sir,' said the Chief Flight Attendant. On landing, we headed straight to Newcastle Police Station and met the local Detective Inspector who allocated two trainee detectives to do all the work for us. It turned out there were loads of blokes in Newcastle who fitted our description. If we couldn't find our man, we'd have to take one at random, which wouldn't be ideal.

We left local officers to track our suspect down, while we had a liquid lunch. A few hours later he was in custody. We called our Freemason DI in London. He said we'd done well so could have a night out at the Commissioner's expense. Two colleagues would fly up to collect Mr Big Geordie and return him south.

He was a big lad with a fondness for steroids, a little volatile. With the help of local uniform, we would need first to get him to the airport and then hand him over, while keeping him calm. That was important. It was at the pilot's discretion whether he would take a prisoner in handcuffs. If Mr Big Geordie wouldn't play ball, our Bigg Market knees-up was out the window and I'd already bought a new miniskirt and killer heels.

As I waited with him for an airport officer to drive us there I began singing gentle lullabies, which he seemed to like. But once the officer arrived, things took a downward turn. Glancing at him in the rearview mirror she said, 'Ooh, I've never had a murderer in the back of my car before!' He got a little incensed about this, but began to relax again once I broke into 'Wheels on the Bus'.

In fact, he had tears in his eyes as we handed him over to the two London detectives who were, quite frankly, rude.

Jealousy is a terrible thing.

And so to Bromley, South London – or in Kent as it prefers to be known – and what appeared to be a burglary gone wrong. Do burglaries ever go right? Is there a sliding scale? Well, this one had gone very wrong indeed.

A man had died.

The local Detective Inspector was at the scene. He showed me his brand of cigarettes and called me son. He'd had a fag in the crime scene and dropped the butt. He thought it okay just to show me his fag packet to be eliminated from our enquiries. Calling him daddio I said we'd be in touch before sauntering off in a threatening way. I wanted to make him sweat.

The victim had a number of rather niche porn videos, so one line of enquiries led to a 'legitimate video outlet' on the south coast. I went down there to take a statement and produced my warrant card at the door, which somehow caused Benny Hill levels of scantily clad women to run out the back of the building. The owner argued that it was perfectly normal to employ a cleaning firm who sent staff in bondage gear. He denied all knowledge of a video production called *Sluts with Nuts* and couldn't for the life of him explain why he owned the PO Box. I left him to have a good long hard look in the mirror.

The filth line of enquiry proved fruitless, so we went down the line of doing an investigation. It is standard practice to do an anniversary witness appeal. This is where coppers hang around looking for people who might have witnessed a violent murder without realising. This is not to be confused with reassurance patrols, which is when a murder has happened that nobody knows about until loads of coppers in yellow jackets waddle about, making them frightened to leave their own homes.

The pathologist reckoned the victim had died in the early hours of the morning, so our appeal needed to take place at the same time. The Freemason DI decided that it would only need two officers, so he chose two lads who were close friends. The victim's road was quite rural. Not much happened during the day, let alone at night. Our boys had to stimulate each other to stay awake. Then they heard the sound of a milk float. It turned out the milkman had actually been out and about the previous week and seen two men on high-powered motorbikes at the end of the victim's drive. He knew what kind of bikes they were as he liked to ride really fast after driving really slowly all day at work.

And they were smoking fags.

This was a key line of enquiry. I phoned the local DI, who still insisted on calling me son to tell him the suspect had been smoking, then stayed silently on the line while he nervously asked questions. I then hung up without saying goodbye.

The detective in charge of exhibits had grabbed all the fag butts on the driveway. Following the discovery of our new witness, they were sent to the lab to be tested for DNA. We had a hit. A local man had been charged with drink-driving a few months previously. His DNA had been taken and put on the database. Now we had his DNA on a fag butt at the scene of a murder where the suspect had been seen smoking.

So one morning we arrested our new suspect. It turned out that he was getting a lift to work from his girlfriend because he'd lost his licence. He'd had a morning smoke, then flicked the butt out the window. In one of the greatest twists of fate in drink-drive ban smoking history, his butt landed in a murder scene. 'What are the odds on that?' I said to his sobbing girlfriend. 'I'm serious. Do you know? I'm banned from William Hill.'

The milkman's knowledge of high-powered motorbikes proved to be the lead that found us the two real suspects. They were convicted and sent down for a fairly long time. All thanks to two detectives stimulating each other in a quiet country lane.

Sometimes things just seem too good to be true, don't they? Well, here's a story to top off my time dealing with killin' south of the river.

We'd been moved into the newly-built Sutton Police Station. Us hardened murder squad detectives had half the building, with special doors to stop the normal coppers getting to us. We got to swagger around their bit though, so they got to call us tossers when we pushed in front in the canteen queue.

We were often expected to stray to the dank corners of London. This usually happened when more local murder teams were 'too busy' or washing their hair or something. The big bosses would decide which Senior Investigating Officer had annoyed them most that month, then send him or her and team to deal with the latest case.

Which is how we ended up in South East London, a god-forsaken part of the world and somewhere I will never holiday. A woman had been found brutally murdered in her flat.

I've always wondered why we feel the need to describe murders as brutal, by the way. I don't remember any being gentle and caring. Murder tends to be exactly what it says on the tin – quick-drying clear varnish.

Anyway, following her discovery, someone called the police. As they have a habit of doing. The local uniformed officers attended and made a right old meal of things. They'd actually done some detecting rather than just putting up a load of crime scene tape and standing there for hours waiting for the detectives to swan in on overtime. The victim's tower block neighbours were spoken to and one recalled hearing something that sounded like a scream in the early hours. It looked like that might have been our victim coming to her premature end.

It turned out the woman had been in a relationship with a violent man who took out his inadequacies on her. And in fact he had been arrested only the week before her death for hanging her over the balcony by her ankles.

Officers viewed CCTV covering the communal entrance and, by Jove, there he was, seen going into the block then leaving some forty-five minutes later. This was more or less around the time the neighbour had heard the scream.

As you would expect, the officers considered this a decent enough lead and went forth and multiplied. They got a group of colleagues together and arrested the boyfriend. He loudly protested his innocence as cowards, nonces and other general wrong-uns tend to do while being nicked.

As the court system no longer takes the word of a police officer as gospel, we needed to do a bit of work. The suspect was interviewed. Despite the interview team screaming, 'You did it! You fucking killed her didn't you?' at him a lot, he insisted on telling us we had the wrong man. He admitted to being on CCTV and said he'd gone there to make up for hanging her over the balcony the week before. We noticed he didn't have petrol station flowers, though, so didn't believe a word of it.

He said he'd knocked, but there had been no answer, so he sat waiting for her a bit, before leaving. A likely story! So someone got onto the CPS to get authority to charge him. They agreed, without being too arsey for a change.

Then everything changed. A man called 999 to let the police know that he hated the police, didn't trust any of us, before going on to tell us that his friend had popped round to see him and asked to stay for a bit. And this friend was covered in blood. The caller's suspicions were further raised when the friend started washing blood off a knife in the kitchen sink while complaining about a woman he'd been on a date with.

Well, that certainly put the cat among the pigeons! The dear old Territorial Support Group were sent round to invite him to assist with our enquires by smashing the door down and piling in on top of him in their riot romper suits.

Someone then had another look at the CCTV and found our new suspect going into the block and leaving twenty minutes or so before the bloke we'd just charged with the murder went in. Turned out our first suspect had been telling the truth all along! He was still a prick though, so we dragged our heels letting him go and left him in the white paper suit, so vigilantes could chase after him when he got outside.

The forensic people went into the flat and took loads of samples of stuff which proved the blood belonged to our victim. They left signed exhibit labels around to show where they'd taken stuff, like the pipe under the sink.

After they'd finished, we got some specially trained search officers in to scour the flat for more evidence. I was tasked with bagging and tagging everything they found and making a written record. Boring! I was cheered up by one of the officers whose day job was on the TSG. He kept telling me he'd found police exhibit labels everywhere. And he wasn't joking.

10

Call Me Sarge and Attending Morning Prayers

After a few years on the Murder Squad, I had it decided for me that it was time to move on.

Before leaving Hammersmith, I'd passed the Sergeants exam. We had to buy books about the so-called law and learn it without the benefit of cartoons. Different level. A lot of the stuff you needed to learn bore little relevance to murder investigations. Like the legislation around lights on skips, or the crap about it being illegal to serve alcohol to a police officer in uniform.

(It's an interesting fact that the CID plain clothes department was formed expressly to bypass this legislation in 1921, as I wrote in answer to question 17.)

Anyway, I got through the exam and the qualification lasted five years, so I immersed myself in dead bodies for a while. When it was nearly time up, I went to see DISCO BISCUIT and told him I was thinking of putting in for promotion. He asked if I needed him out the way so I could get the Hoover under his desk. I felt moved that he thought I was the office cleaner. He'd always denied knowing me at all before then.

The application form asked me to confirm that I had never been involved in terrorist activities or efforts to undermine the economic wellbeing of the UK. They weren't letting that one go.

There was a box for 'any other comments'. I wrote, 'Give me promotion or the fucking budgie gets it,' signed it in blood and added a few feathers for dramatic effect. A lot of HR types are twitchers in their spare time.

Long story short, I was soon elevated to the rank of Detective Sergeant within the Metropolitan Police Service and accidentally applied to be sent to the London Borough of Lambeth. Lambeth features Brixton, which never stops giving. It was heavily policed following rioting in reaction to heavy policing in the 1980s.

My posting was Kennington Police Station, to the north of the Borough, which is like Brixton but with more flats belonging to Members of Parliament. And knocking shops. There was a massive disparity between wealth and poverty, which made it much easier to know where to heavily police.

Fortunately I didn't move to Lambeth alone. Another member of the Murder squad, a product of Cornwall or Devon or possibly both, was promoted too. He couldn't understand electricity.

Our new Borough came in three parts. Kennington at the top, Brixton in the middle and Streatham, where I wouldn't choose to go if my life depended on it. Each site had its own Senior Management Team, in fierce competition with each other. It was almost as if their own promotional prospects depended on it.

At Kennington most senior officers were instantly forgettable. There was one uniformed Chief Inspector called Major Cock, I think, who pursued the higher rank with religious zeal. He wore his trousers tight to attract attention from people with an interest in his future, the sort of man who ate meat from a tin with a soup spoon. I was posted to the CID side, in line to be managed by a series of Detective Inspectors. As a Detective Sergeant, I got to call them by their first names, even though I wasn't their mother.

The DCI was very keen on himself. He was on the High Potential Development Scheme, which says it all, and renowned for his ability to make any conversation about himself. Senior Management Teams were generally full of people with limited self-awareness, so he fitted right in.

Coming from the Murder Squad, the West Country lad and I thought it would be a good idea to email the DCI and tell him how bloody important we were. The DCI didn't take this well and posted us to the Case Progression Unit, where you deal with prisoners the uniformed response team bring in. For shame!

My CPU team comprised uniformed response officers who'd irritated Sergeants. We would deal with all the prisoners that didn't fall within the remit of the Main Office CID, as defined by the detectives in the Main Office CID, ie all of them.

Lambeth Borough had the highest emergency call demand in London, which led to a load of motorists being persecuted and people arrested for all sorts of offences. If the CPU felt a little overwhelmed by it all, I was instructed to seek support from the uniformed Duty Inspector but only made this mistake once. I've never felt so degraded. On a positive note, I picked up a few tips for use in my later Duty Inspector years when dealing with Detective Sergeants who were twats.

Kennington was my first taste of leadership and I supped deeply from a cup of authoritarian tendencies that I didn't know I had.

Much had changed since my last foray into Borough Policing at Hammersmith. The officers under my command seemed to be more interested in going to the gym than spending every waking hour in the pub. They appeared to have swallowed the

Commissioner's blue pill that 'integrity is non-negotiable'. I went to the pub with my former Murder Squad colleague. We swore together that there would be changes and that we were the men to drive them. Then he got spooked by an exploding light bulb, ran off, and hasn't been seen since.

One of my first tasks in the CPU was to have a formal chat with an officer. I had received an email complaining that he'd been asked loads of times to type out an interview transcript and hadn't done it. It turned out that as his supervisor I would have to address the issue. Who knew?

I had no idea what to do, but decided to follow the creed that had thus far served me well – make it up as you go along.

I planned to speak to him in private, so the rest of the office didn't heckle or throw paper clips. I would offer words of advice and leave it as an informal resolution, written note on his file. Or, if he got arsey, I might just shout at the prick.

I walked into the office attempting to look nonchalant. Harder than it sounds. There were three police Constables tapping away on computers. Our reluctant typist was filing his nails.

'Morning,' I said, nonchalantly. He carried on filing. Perhaps I needed to work on my voice projection, so I yelled his name a little hysterically. He knocked coffee into his lap and leapt to his feet. The other two pretended nothing was going on. I imagine they thought I might start smashing computers up.

I asked the culprit for a word. He nodded and called me Sarge, so I puffed my chest out. 'Be afraid. Be very afraid,' I said, as I led him to a little office down the corridor, a dumping ground for broken chairs, desks and dreams, and closed the door assertively. I asked if he wanted to sit down, but with all the furniture being knackered he had to stay on his feet. Then a light bulb popped, (another one, we had a few) and we were suddenly in darkness.

'It's about the tape transcript,' I said. 'There's been an email.'

'I haven't had a chance, Sarge,' he said. 'There's so much to do I'm feeling overwhelmed. I can't sleep for thinking about work.'

'I don't want to hear no excuses,' I replied. 'You're either in my tent pissing out or outside pissing in on me,' my messaging ideally judged to reinforce the vision and values of the Met.

Then I heard crying. Bollocks. We hadn't covered sobbing Police Constables on the Sergeants course.

I had to improvise. He was a young lad with a long life ahead of him, so I felt paternal. He needed consoling. I reached out to rest a reassuring hand on his shoulder, but mistimed in the dark and slapped the side of his head. He started sobbing even harder and made snotty gulping sounds.

I managed to take his hand and opened the door into the glare of the corridor, where Major Cock was at that very moment doing a few lunges. He had a quizzical look on his face, either wondering what I was doing leaving a darkened room holding hands with a sobbing PC, or having twisted a testicle.

I tapped the side of my head and did that thing where you twirl your finger around to suggest mental breakdown.

It wasn't the first time I'd made somebody cry. While on the Murder Squad once, I arrested a chap on suspicion of murder. There he stood, all wobbly-lipped, in his Arsenal top. 'Okay,' I said, attempting to lighten the mood a little. 'You're under arrest for murder – and also being an Arsenal fan.'

'There is a time and a place Byrne, you twat!' said the angry Welsh DS with me, as he helped the man, completely distraught, back to his feet. Later it turned out he hadn't killed anyone after all. He *was* an Arsenal fan, though, so there was that.

After serving my sentence with uniformed officers, I was allowed to escape and rejoin the CID whose offices were upstairs, an extra hurdle for uniformed officers as they tried to hand in prisoners.

I put a sign up at the bottom of the stairs that read, 'Don't bother' but they still gave it a go. Bless.

Here, the CID was split into two: Main Officer and Priority

Crime Unit. I was thrust into the PCU, who dealt with robberies and burglaries and were expected to aid the promotion prospects of senior officers by massaging figures. Crimes were 'cleared up' by charge, caution or the laughable 'Taken Into Consideration'. This meant that when someone was in trouble for breaking and entering, they could admit to other offences. The police would then write a nice letter to the Judge requesting that he or she be lenient on the accused.

TICs were often the difference between hitting targets or not and were very popular with the Senior Management Team.

For obvious reasons.

Everyone in custody for burglary would be offered the once in a lifetime opportunity to drive around with detectives to point out all the offences they'd done. It never ceased to amaze me how often drug-addicted burglars could remember the hundreds of premises they'd stolen from. Some detectives very kindly assisted such characters by printing out long lists for them to sign.

Once upon a time, a committed burglar fancied a day out from prison so made contact with Brixton PCU, who made haste to his side. He then had a lovely three days at Brixton Police Station, with regular outings to visit friends. Having eventually admitted to several hundred burglary offences, a future doing his memory act in Las Vegas surely awaited.

Before long, Kennington senior sorts got wind of it. As a DS in the PCU, I should be getting my supervisors' evidence for *their* promotions, apparently, not letting Brixton have all the glory. I gave my opposite number at Brixton a call. He kept hanging up, so I drove over.

The PCU at Brixton was on the ground floor, so I managed to have a conversation through the window. As detectives in a conflict situation most of this involved saying, 'You fucking what?' a few times, until a DCI leant out of an upstairs window and told us to leave it fucking out. It turned out that despite admitting to several hundred burglary offences in the Brixton area, this particular miscreant was refusing to admit to anything north of the sub-Divisional Police boundary with Kennington. Remarkable that, I thought, as some uniform escorted me off the premises. The Senior Management Team (SMUT) at Kennington were incandescent with rage when they discovered I'd 'solved' exactly zero burglaries. I wasn't fussed. Fiddling figures is bent.

NB: In 2014 the National Statistics Agency said, 'There is accumulating evidence that suggests underlying data on crimes recorded by the police may not be reliable.'

As a PCU supervisor, I would sometimes have to represent the Detective Inspector at the Morning Management Meeting, otherwise known as Morning Prayers.

This was when the Senior Management Team (SMUT) would deploy the power of hindsight to criticise the work of everyone else in the last twenty-four hours, and bemoan any perceived lack of figures to support their next promotion.

Morning Prayers was often chaired by Major Cock, who as he entered the room would ignore anyone with no influence on promotion prospects before sitting, legs splayed. I'm convinced he used raw chicken breasts in a way God never intended.

He also took delight in mocking and belittling junior officers, often turning his ire on the PCU, especially when there'd been a load of robberies overnight. I did argue that I hadn't personally been out doing the robberies, but he insisted on planting the blame firmly on me. Little did he know I was flicking the Vs at him behind my clipboard.

Kennington had a number of active gang members, who always seemed to be falling out with each other over some trifle or other. As the police, we were expected to do something about this. On one occasion, a car full of gang chaps was stopped by uniformed officers. They were on their way to Wandsworth, the neighbouring Borough, to have some beef or something.

The uniform searched the car and found an AK47 in a JD Sports bag. A dangerous weapon and evidence of poor clothing choices. The bag was in the boot and all four occupants denied knowing anything about it, which is just typical.

So the gang guys were brought back to Kennington and had a right sulk in a cell. The arresting officers made sure the weapon was safe by firing it into the roof until it stopped going bang.

I was the Duty Detective Sergeant, so got to be really sarcastic when the officers came to tell me about the case. I told them they were lucky to be alive, which went down as well as you'd imagine. I agreed to take the case, but did a yawn and rolled my eyes before waving them out of the PCU office with a fey hand.

I grabbed my weeping colleague from the CPU to help me interview the suspects, determined to assist his progression into CID, whether he liked it or not. I felt guilty about making him cry in a darkened room, especially in front of CI Major Cock.

The first interview went well. The front seat passenger admitted to shopping in JD Sports and apologised profusely. He wasn't having anything to do with the AK47 though. I put it to him that travelling in the front passenger seat, 'riding shotgun', suggested he knew full well there was a shooter in the booter. His solicitor got a bit tetchy about my rhyming stylee and told me I was being unprofessional. I did a blubbery fart to indicate to her exactly what being unprofessional was and left the room, closing the door exactly like DI Burnside from *The Bill*.

I'd done my research, determined to cut off any line of defence, and got confirmation from the sports shop that they did not stock Kalashnikovs (Russian: Автома́т Кала́шникова), gas-operated assault rifles chambered for 7.62×39mm cartridges. They did however have a special offer on Converse high tops.

Next up, I interviewed the driver, who claimed he'd just hired the car and hadn't checked the boot. I'd anticipated this as well, well on the way to becoming Best Detective of the Week at this rate. The car rental place too confirmed that it did not include gas-operated assault rifles as optional extras in its hire vehicles, although presumably it would frown on any scratches caused by shootouts. The driver was in a corner and I was painting the floor with a big police brush. The AK must have been left there by the previous user, he said, and I took all the evidence to the Crown Prosecution Service (CUPS).

When I first joined, the police were allowed to make charging decisions, halcyon days for performance figures. Senior officers could demand a person be charged and by golly they were. Then some public school Home Office type decided this was poor form and said the Crown Prosecution Service should take over.

The CPS made the least popular lawyer in the office go and sit in the local police station to deal with the officers. I saw this duty lawyer and he looked petrified, either imagining I'd brought the AK47 with me or noticing I had just had my mullet frothed. After a bit of horseplay, the CPS agreed to charge and a decision was made to let the suspects stay overnight with us before giving them a lift to court next day.

After which my crying colleague and I went to The Pineapple, a favourite local haunt. Like the police station, it opened 24 hours a day for coppers. Major Cock often demanded licencing laws be enforced there, because he didn't have any friends. And some years later, it would appear on page one of the *London Evening Standard* under the headline: '[Four police] had sex with woman in pub lavatory.' The allegations were probed by Scotland Yard.

Next morning, I went to Morning Prayers, again hosted by Major Cock, legs so far apart I had to squeeze into a chair in the corner. It had been a good session in The Pineapple, interrupted only by uniform driving by with the theme to *The Sweeney* on the tannoy. We had to lob a few pint pots to get them to piss off.

After a night duty emergency response critique by way of an aperitif, team Cock got down to business. He wanted to know why there'd been a sharp rise in robbery allegations. Everyone stared at me, even though I was whistling and looking out the window. Cock clicked his poultry-scented fingers in my face. I said we'd been busy locking up armed criminals and taken an AK47 off the street. My photos posing with it were on Facebook.

This wasn't good enough for the Cockmeister, who threw a printout at me that landed short, so I had to pick it off the floor. He'd been rubbing his boots on his balls again, I noted. They were nice and shiny.

A load of muggings had been taken place at a cashpoint opposite Lambeth underground. Minutes from Kennington Police Station, a series of violent robberies had nevertheless taken place there against young women taking out cash. Some suffered serious injury, dragged down the street by two assailants. Both had knives and seemed keen to use them at any sign of resistance.

Old Cocky-chops wanted the robberies solved toot suite. He made a number of disparaging comments about police officers who weren't him and then left the room like someone bobbing in and out of toilet cubicles when the toilet roll has run out.

Due to the high level of violence, I opted to get our old friends in the TSG to assist us. An office Johnnie with a power complex would decide which part of London needed the fighting feds the most. I wrote an application designed to appeal to the TSG:

Their has bin muggin in south. Bad men. Big knife. WUMAN! TSG fight! Hit bad men. Home Office approve tactics. Overtime. Yes, mate!
Respectfully submitted for consideration,
Detective Sergeant Paul Byrne BPhil (6 mon)

Should it prove operationally necessary, the TSG could operate in plain clothes. Inspectors and Sergeants were authorised to dress themselves and carry out lower level surveillance against people who wouldn;t notice twenty-one Millwall fans following them around in Raybans getting grown-ups to do their shoelaces. My bid was successful, a phrase I rarely, if ever, used during my police career. I had an entire team of TSG officers to take down the cashpoint robbers. I would need to give a briefing and give out individual roles in simple language with lots of colourful cartoons. I was careful not to do or say anything that might spark their intermittent explosive anger disorder.

The day of the operation came. We had an observation point (OP) overlooking the target area. This was staffed by a male and female member of the TSG. The rest would lurk around local sidestreets waiting for the OP to tell them to run around and batter people. They were all pumped up and eager to go after the briefing, which was a pleasant surprise. They were clearly keen to lock up the bad guys. Or it was the steroids. Difficult to tell.

I stayed in the office and monitored the police radio channel the TSG were using, hearing a series of strange noises and grunts. I worried they'd accidentally been taken captive at Vauxhall City Zoo. It wouldn't take them long to go native, if so.

After about an hour, all hell broke loose, which is really ace when it happens in the police. Less so following the Rapture as foretold in the Book of Revelation.

A photogenic young woman was taking out some cash, so I knew there'd be media interest. Two men sprinted over the road and attacked her. Then the TSG got medieval on their asses. One was arrested at the scene, the other ran a short way until deciding to fight the riot feds outside a restaurant. I'm not revealing any sensitive information by saying fighting the TSG after mugging a photogenic woman isn't the best idea. The TSG then came back to the station with their prisoners and 'wrote' their statements.

I can only applaud the honesty of the female officer who said, in her official police statement, that when the suspects attacked the victim, and the call to 'GO GO GO' was given, she was in the toilet. I imagined the future court case:

Barrister for the baddies: 'And officer, can you tell the members of the jury where exactly you were when my clients allegedly committed this so-called robbery?'

Officer: 'I was 'aving a shit M'Lud.'

Judge: 'I'm sorry, what?'

Barrister: 'The officer was defecating, Your Honour.'

Judge: 'Fuck me backwards. Continue.'

I made sure I was able to attend Morning Prayers the next day to soak in the adoration of the Senior Leaders. Major Cock was in the chair again and rather flustered. I hoped the rash had come back, but it turned out he was really upset about one of the witnesses listed on the crime report. Which he threw at me.

A Labour MP had been dining in the restaurant when his reverie was disturbed by the riot police using reasonable force to batter fuck out of a mugger. 'Get a fucking statement off him this morning,' the Cockster ordered, in a panic.

'Of course, but we need to arrange the ID parades first and...'
'He's a fucking leftie. He'll be well anti.'

By this, CI Major Cock meant that because our witness was a Labour MP, he was naturally left-wing, which to him meant he would be against the police. Cock suspected the MP might give a negative statement that would lead to the suspect's release. This would impact performance figures... etc. He offered no interest in the victim, no praise for the TSG or PSU officers.

Anyway, I got a statement from the MP, went to the Houses Of Parliament and got stared at by Iain Duncan Smith. The MP gave a statement full of praise for police actions and offered to appear in court to support the officers and their justifiable use of force. What a nice man.

I'd experience Major Cock again many years later at a briefing centre for Notting Hill Carnival. By then he'd been promoted several times and was strutting like a peacock with chicken breasts down its trousers. He had staff officers and other groupies to write stuff down and take his photograph.

He ignored me, but clearly needed a wee. One of his staff asked me where the senior officer toilets were, in a really sarcastic way. I said we had an agreement with the Rampage Sound System allowing very senior officers to have a piss at the back of their stage and chuckled quietly as Major Cock scuttled off to cause a breakdown in community relations via the medium of urine.

Intestines All Over the Shop and Showing High Potential

I never forgot my roots as a uniformed constable on an emergency response team. It's the key role in policing, and where you're most likely to do really stupid things that nobody thanks you for.

I appreciated the PCU had to maintain a good relationship with the uniform and took the time to praise the actions of the initial responders in Morning Prayers, which made the other attendees look at me like I had Ebola.

In one meeting I pointed out that the emergency response uniformed Duty Officer and I were wearing the same socks. It was a way of reaching out across the divide. He just looked at me without speaking. I think he was touched. Deep down.

My relationship building with the uniform really helped one morning in Kennington.

There had been nasty robberies on a bus. The suspect could clearly be seen on CCTV using a knife to threaten his cowering victims. The stills were circulated as part of our investigation. Two of my team immediately identified him as a well-known criminal from a local estate.

'That's Robber McRobberface!' said PC Bill.

'Yes, that's definitely Robber McRobberface!' agreed PC Ben.

That was enough for me. Two seasoned street cops had made a firm identification. We would go early the next morning and bring him to justice. Our friends in uniform would wait outside in the police van. We would get the arrest, bung him in a cell, then nip over the road for breakfast. Sweet.

And the day started off as planned. We climbed the stairs to his third-floor flat, PC Bill tasked with making the arrest. We would knock, introduce ourselves and ask Mr McRobberface to assist us with our enquires down the station. Simple.

We knocked. Mr McRobberface's mother answered the door. She was rather annoyed when she realised her peace was being disturbed by her local police service. She made her feelings clear in a profanity-ridden diatribe. I would have liked to suggest that maybe her son's hobby of being a violent mugger might have something to do with the regular attendance of Her Majesty's finest, but this might have had a negative impact on her customer satisfaction survey, so I bit my tongue.

McRobberface came to the door. He was somewhat calmer than his mother. He asked what we wanted.

'Are you Robber McRobberface?' enquired PC Bill.

It was a question we all knew the answer to, but we'd learned our trade from the cops on TV. We intended to put a hand on his head when putting him in the back of the police van as well. McRobberface didn't answer. It had been a stupid question in all fairness. 'Right. You're under arrest for burglary.'

Burglary?

'Bill you silly old so-and-so! It's robbery! He's to be arrested for robbery, you daftie!' I said. I would have used more profanity, but PC Bill wanted to go to Special Branch and was sensitive.

'Burglary! Fucking burglary? I ain't a fucking burglar!' The once calm and relaxed McRobberface suddenly transformed into an extremely angry man. It seemed his worldview found violent knife-point robbery perfectly acceptable, but breaking into houses! It was like we'd accused him of being a kiddie fiddler.

And then he produced a knife from a table by the door. I assumed it was his robbin' knife he'd dropped there with his keys on getting home. He came out the door, slashing at us, seemingly trying to stab us to death for calling him a housebreaker. The rest of his family poured out and got stuck in as well.

We ended up milling with the angry householders. I managed to call for assistance on the radio while dancing backwards down the stairs with McRobberface. I doubt he knew that the last person who'd tried to stab me ended up with his testicles in his throat. He was playing Russian Roulette with his gonads.

I managed to force the knife out of his hand and threw it out a window. He insisted on trying to headbutt me in the face and managed to smear hair wax across my glasses. My world became a blurry foxtrot with an incensed mugger who insisted on leading. We were saved by the uniformed officers in the van, who kindly decided to investigate why the DS was lobbing hunting knives out of windows and screaming like a dickhead.

McRobberface was sentenced to three months in prison for attacking us with a knife and smearing my glasses.

He was never charged with the bus robberies, though. I shall leave the reasons for this to the autobiographies of both PC Bill and PC Ben. For shame. It took weeks to get the hair grease off my glasses too. When I could finally see again, it turned out I'd been moved to the Main Office CID.

The Main Office dealt with everything that couldn't be batted back to uniform to deal with. Which meant very little, to be honest. It also had a balcony overlooking the station yard, so you could flick cigarette butts onto Chief Inspector Major Cock while he was outside for a strut.

I would now be fulfilling the role of Duty Detective Sergeant. I got to roll up at crime scenes, expect the PCs to lift the crime scene tape up for me, and call everyone 'son'.

As we very rarely took over cases from uniform, we'd be lumbered dealing with prisoners from non-local units. These were pan-London types who'd come to Lambeth to annoy me and included police dogs, firearms officers and the TSG. So pawprints, crayons and dribble, in essence.

If someone got arrested by a dog, things hadn't gone well. The dog wouldn't actually made the arrest. They usually had their mouths full, so couldn't do the caution. The handler would come up to the office and hand over the prisoner. We didn't argue, in case he got his dog to rip our arms off. I was always keen to joke about expecting a statement from the dog. The handlers would give me that look that suggested they thought I was a twat. They wouldn't say it out loud due to respect for rank.

I didn't joke with the firearms officers, especially the ones on medication.

The TSG. We had to suffer their prisoner handovers fairly often. They'd run up the stairs (obviously) shouting, 'Attack! Attack! Attack!' and always kept their hats on indoors. They couldn't deal with their own prisoners due to their general levels of literacy. Or in case they were required to make a bad situation worse somewhere else in London on the hurry up.

As a Detective Sergeant, it was my responsibility to be as rude and condescending to the TSG as possible. Other DSs across London have extended this to everyone they ever meet, but I'm a liberal so just riled the Thick and Stupid Group. I knew just how far you could push a TSG PC before they'd explode and rip you out of your suit before trying to drown you by shoving your head down a toilet bowl.

Despite my efforts, we had a fairly steady workload. I'd been lumbered with Bill and Ben so had two people to give all the work to. They'd nearly had me killed with their dodgy identifications of muggers, so I felt it was time they gave something back. I took 25 per cent of their overtime payments.

One day a young chap was minding his own business on a bus. He'd paid his fare, which can often be seen as a sign of weakness. Proper hard lads just give it the stare at the driver, who pretends he's all scared, but really can't be arsed with silly little boys trying to gangsta walk up the stairs.

Another man, of around the same age gets on. Let's call him the suspect. He went straight upstairs and headed straight for the back seats. The sign of a true hard man.

Our chap looked up at him and nodded. Let's call him the victim, without giving too much of the plot away. The suspect then produced a hunting knife and disembowelled our victim. For nodding at him. CCTV showed the victim slumped in his seat, holding his intestines. The suspect then got off the bus not having travelled anywhere. Nobody stopped him. All the other passengers developed a sudden interest in their shoes.

Doctors and nurses saved the victim's life, but he left the hospital with some choice words for the police. He wasn't going to co-operate. Can't say I blame him to be honest. I had first hand experience of what the police were like.

In really serious cases, the police can proceed without the support of the victim. By this time, I was a seasoned Detective Sergeant, so was able to tell what was serious and what wasn't. I told Bill and Ben to clear their diaries. This was a big job. We needed to find this suspect before he did it again. He'd tried to kill someone for nodding. God knows what he'd do if someone blew him a kiss.

An appeal went out in the local press but I wasn't holding my breath. I'd seen the CCTV. I wouldn't want to get on the wrong side of him, either, and that was something I was paid to do. Imagine if you were his yoga instructor?

Then someone called in. I can't name them here for their own safety, but can confirm it wasn't a yoga instructor. I don't want the blood of a yogini on my mat.

We were told who our suspect was and where he lived. I gathered Bill and Ben and told them we had an arrest enquiry to do, then recalled how they'd nearly had me killed so changed the 'we' to 'you'. The Detective Inspector stuck his oar in. Apparently, trainee Detectives were not there to be 'sacrificed'. I needed to use the TSG. Not sure I agreed, but that's the rank structure in a disciplined organisation for you. I put a bid in for the TSG:

> Big red buss. Ding! Ding! Badman see nice man nod KNIFE! Bloode! Oh, god the bloode! TSG go fetch! Good boy! Good boy! Fetch the baddie!
> *Respectfully submitted for consideration,*
> *Detective Sergeant Paul Byrne BPhil (Toilet paper)*

The TSG bit my hand off. Not literally. They got to dress up and put on their big helmets and use sledgehammers and shields. They asked a postman to show them the right address so arrested the right person. I whispered a prayer of relief. Getting the right man wasn't as common as you might think. One of the TSG found a bag with a blood-covered knife in it. I gave them all stickers for being brave soldiers.

The suspect was trussed up and taken to Kennington Police Station, where he was put in a cell and had his clothes taken. This was for evidential purposes, not a critique of his style choices. Instead, he had to wear one of those white paper suits that became fashionable with leading rapists in the 1970s, much to the distress of painters and decorators.

A solicitor arrived from a local firm and I sat down with her for a chat using my best telephone voice, so she didn't consider me uncouth. I'd done my research and found out that the suspect had previously stabbed a solicitor in the eye with a pen. Even though she was wearing glasses, she was somewhat concerned about this. We agreed that she could speak to him through the cell wicket, rather than sit in a private room where he'd be offered a pen to sign paperwork. I didn't want to tempt fate.

Some TSG officers stood down the corridor in case the suspect launched an attack on his solicitor. I suggested they wear earmuffs so they couldn't hear the legally privileged conversation between lawyer and client, but the TSG sergeant told me to piss off and called me the C-word.

I led the interview and another officer sat in with me. I'd managed to catch him just as he was leaving through a second-floor window. In a slight change to protocol, I sat behind this colleague instead of next to him as was standard. If pens started flying, I wanted a human shield. The suspect didn't speak, not even to say, 'no comment'. He stared at me without blinking, while rubbing his dick through his paper suit. I had to proceed with all my questioning, despite the suspect appearing to pleasure himself. I didn't draw attention to his revolting actions in case he dug out the other officer's eyes with a Biro.

In the end, all went to plan and he was sent to prison for loads of years. He is probably out now, though, so I've subsequently moved house in case he wants to progress the relationship.

After recovering from being an object of lust to a psychopath, I found out I was expected to do Night Duties. Nights saw most detectives tucked up in bed. A smattering were required to work through the wee small hours to ensure there was always someone on hand to criticise the actions of the uniformed response team. This was a holding position – The Hindsight Police deployed the following meeting at Morning Prayers.

As Night Duty DS I was told I had responsibility for the whole

Borough of Lambeth supported by six Detective Constables, two at each station.

One set of nights, I was accompanied by a female officer who'd somehow managed to join the CID without working in uniform. I suspect she was connected. I'd seen *Goodfellas*, so knew how those things worked. I phoned up the detectives at Brixton and Streatham to make sure they were sinking under the volume of work, then went for a drive around. CID cars don't have police markings, so mad people can't wave them down. We were always recognised as police officers driving around Brixton. People would shout, 'Five-O' at us and rock the car at traffic lights.

Like a mug, I often tried to help out uniform when they dealt with calls. This often surprised the Control Room, because CID taking a call is as rare as rocking horse shite. One night I took one in Brixton and headed down with my colleague.

A local resident had heard smashing glass and looked outside. They'd seen a white man with no top on smash the front window of a car. He was trying to get in. They called the police for some unknown reason. We turned up and there he still was. Just as described, exactly where he should be, next to the car he was accused of trying to steal. Case closed indeed. I walked towards him like a boss, flicked my warrant card and gave it the large.

Something didn't seem right, though. He didn't look like your typical car thief. I checked my prejudices. He was toned. Well built and good looking. I checked my sexuality. I used my gruff cop voice and asked what his game was.

Something about his body language, a slightly crouched pose, made me suspect he was extremely dangerous. He said, 'Who the fuck are you?' in an Australian accent. I moved back a little, remembered that my colleague in the car had the radio but didn't know how to use it' due to having missed working in uniform.

I said, 'police' in one of those really weedy voices you used at school before bullies kicked your head in. He didn't seem pacified. In fact, he seemed to be getting angry. After making sure our car was all locked and secured, my oppo sauntered up. She'd heard about cars getting broken into, I supposed, and didn't want to risk anyone nicking our packed lunches.

I told her: 'As soon as I say run, you go as fast as your legs will carry you, find a grown-up and tell them your Detective Sergeant is in almighty big trouble. Then tell them to get ma and pa, gather the mules and bring pitchforks. You hear me now, as Jesus is my witness?'

'Christ, you're a prick,' she replied.

And then the local area car arrived in all its uniformed glory. My god, I wept, thank you! Thank you! The driver looked at me like she'd never seen a grown Detective Sergeant cry before.

Our man spotted the uniform and seemed to relax. Not the traditional reaction of a car thief.

One of the real cops asked what he was doing. And he told us, in what would be the most bizarre outcome of my career.

Our man was Australian Special Forces. He'd been deployed in Iraq and had been given three days rest and recuperation with other members of his unit. They'd been put in a hotel in Brixton. As a really special treat. As young men do, they'd gone heavily on the piss, before getting back to their hotel. Surprisingly, for some of the hardest men in the world, they couldn't take their drink. Our man had got out of bed to use the toilet and managed to lock himself out of his room. He, somehow, had found himself on the streets of Brixton, breaking into a car to sleep.

Sounded like bollocks, but I for one wasn't going to tell him. He had military ID, but no SAS badges, hats or balloons to give away. I was about to rip the piss, then realised he'd probably killed quite a lot of people. We took Mr SAS for a drive around, hoping we could find his hotel during which trip I took the opportunity to give him a personal safety lecture. The part of Brixton he'd wandered into was a mugging hotspot. He'd been a lucky man.

'He's fucking SAS. Who's going to mug him?' my colleague asked. In a pretty damn smug way, I must say.

We were at a loss what to do with him, though, so I thought I'd best seek advice. I'd have to call the uniformed Duty Officer, an Inspector. He was a rank above me, but I was a detective, so there was likely to be conflict.

I was always told when I was Night Duty Detective Sergeant that I was the representative of the Detective Chief Inspector, the senior detective officer on the Borough. These things mattered. I was getting a bit flustered as our passenger kept cracking his knuckles. I worried he might garrotte me from the back seat.

My hands were shaking as I made the call.

'Hello, Duty Officer, Lima Kilo One.'

'Hello. I'm God's representative on earth and I've captured a Special Forces soldier in Brixton, over and out.'

'I'm sorry, what?'

'I am God's representative on earth and I have the SAS in the car and I think he's going to kill me over and out.'

'Is that you, Paul?'

'Yes, sir.'

'Give yourself a bit of space, and do those breathing exercises we talked about, then give me a call back.'

I asked my colleague to do that. He said he'd make some calls. Within minutes, some blokes in a blacked-out van turned up. I told them I'd once had dealings with Mossad and mentioned Floella Benjamin, but they just took my pocket notebook and mobile phone before driving off with Crocodile Dundee.

Having not died at the hands of the Australian Special Forces, I decided to apply for the High Potential Development Scheme. I'd run it past the Detective Chief Inspector. He said, 'Please God, yes. Go for it. Please.' I had his blessing.

I had to write an application form stating why I was a leader of the future. I used to read the comic *2000AD* growing up, so I started with that. For my diversity evidence, I used the case of the man who'd suffocated due to wearing an overtight gimp suit. Edgy. The DCI wrote I was an exceptionally talented supervisor and supported the application with every fibre of his being.

I was summoned to a two-day assessment centre. This turned out to be in a hotel in Bedford. Born in Luton, I took that as a good omen. It was a national assessment, whereby all candidates who'd passed the paper sift would be required to impress self-regarding senior officers of ACPO rank. This stands for the Association of Chief Police Officers. All members are supplied with a mirror and lipstick to give themselves big sloppy kisses.

I arrived at the hotel and decided not to drink heavily. I sat in my room under a rotating ceiling fan, all *Apocalypse Now*. We had to arrive the day before the assessment started. It was all psychological mind games.

The couple in the next room were engaged in games of a different kind. I couldn't believe it. Twice in my career, I had to stay overnight in a hotel prior to a promotion test, and on both occasions, people were shagging in the next room. 'Bummer,' I shouted. 'I'm trying!' replied the man next door.

Next morning, we were addressed by some lackey who spent loads of time explaining the etiquette. We were paid taxpayers' money to kiss the arse of narcissists. That was my take away.

I was forced to interact with other candidates. One northern bloke kept wanting to line up ducks for some reason. There were three Met officers, me Detective Sergeant on Lambeth Borough, in case you've started reading the book at this point. Hi.

There was a Detective Constable from Hackney Borough and a guy without a chin, still at training school. I asked about sex dolls and he looked at me how people from public schools do.

Then we started the assessment. It was all based on business methodology and was, to be honest, utter wank. I struggled to understand how the philosophy of capitalism fitted with looking after people less fortunate. I mentioned it to the chinless trainee, but he told me to polish his shoes and tossed me a shilling.

We were to be assessed by high-ranking officers. Mostly they came from silly little police forces, the sort that are dotted around the country and deal with inbreeding and disputes between cows. They don't come to big cities as people in shoes scare them.

They were called Deputy or Assistant Chief Constables, ranks that don't exist in the Met, so I was all at sea. My philosophy was always: if in doubt, call them ma'am. Can't go wrong that way. Despite being in charge of about ten coppers, they all had staff officers and drivers. A lack of opposable thumbs likely made it hard for them to drive themselves, in fairness.

Each and every one used received punctuation and acted all cultured, but I knew they all lived in their mothers' barns.

One of the exercises involved sitting in a pretend business meeting with other candidates pretending we were high-powered business executives trying to order teenage hookers on a jolly to Bangkok. I think. Or maybe it was tendering for a big contract. There was definitely cocaine involved. The senior officers were trying to assess how assertive we could be, so everyone had to do some shouting and bang on tables. At one point I screamed and tore out clumps of my own hair.

The interview stage was my final downfall. I suggested that random stop and search led to resentment amongst hard to reach communities. The arse interviewing me threw his half-moon specs on the table and began shouting. He wanted to know if there were any more of my boss Sir Ian Blair's policies I disagreed with? Little blokes with inferiority complexes often rise through the ranks so they can shout at people without getting filled in. I'm not violent, but felt like slapping his wig across the room.

I failed the assessment and feedback went to my despairing DCI. I had done so badly, the arsehats suggested I might think about considering a career in another profession.

I found out that applications for Detective Sergeants on the Murder Squad had come out while I'd been away. The DCI had very kindly filled one in for me and sent it off. He wrote that I was an exceptional candidate, and offered his daughter's hand in marriage to the head of Murder HR, a touching endorsement. I was going to be leaving dear old Kennington town.

Once upon a time, in a galaxy far, far away, a young man was sitting at home watching TV. Actually, he was in a flat in Brixton. His flat was in one of the many tower blocks dotted across South London, where the damp was rising and the walls were thin.

Despite his robust use of the volume buttons on his remote controls, he couldn't drown out the thudding and shouting from a neighbouring flat. So he decided to pop next door and have a word, not a decision to be taken lightly in a Brixton tower block.

When the young man stepped from his flat onto the balcony, he was met by the sight of one man straddling another while furiously stabbing him about the face and torso with a very large knife. Most people, quite understandably, would have apologised, made their excuses and left. Like a *News of the World* journalist before a naked politician with a pink bow tied to his penis.

Not this time. Our young man decided he was going to get amongst it. Even though he was wearing slippers and a dressing gown. And he wasn't even pissed.

It now turned into an extended bout as the knifeman decided to turn his anger on the assailant in nightwear. A local grass called the cops, who finally turned up. It took six highly trained coppers with handcuffs and big sticks to restrain the brute.

By which time the debonair neighbour had been stabbed, but he did make a full recovery, as did the man whose life he'd saved. The coppers went in next door's flat and found a corpse. The knifeman had already killed one and was working on the second when the man who couldn't hear his telly got involved.

I love stories of 'ordinary' members of the public getting stuck in and doing incredibly brave things to save lives. A real hero. Not wanting to raise a glass to him would take a heart of stone.

Murder in Belgravia and Becoming a Man of Acton

Having failed to become a leader of the future, and despite being asked to leave the police by the Assistant Chief Constable of Carrotshire, I did then pass an interview for Murder Squad DS.

In this new role I was to be based at Belgravia, in the heart of posh London. Two teams shared the building with uniformed officers who attended to the needs of the Russian oligarchs who owned most of the surrounding streets. I didn't make jokes about this at the time in case of nerve gas.

Belgravia was a designated terrorist station, where criminals arrested by people with guns and wearing balaclavas could stay. Counter Terrorist Command were annoying. They thought they were cleverer than us and had cars whose doors opened upwards, like the DeLorean in *Back to the Future*.

The Murder Squad was led by another DISCO BISCUIT who had astounding levels of self-regard and three DIs under him. I ended up marrying one, a novel departure from my previous experience on the Murder Squad. One was remarkably laid back and the other ex-Flying Squad, which is all you need to know.

I was given line management responsibility for a 'forage' of Detective Constables, none of whom I made cry. I did have to speak to one about an ill-fated imaginary love affair with a younger and more attractive officer. I addressed his deranged fantasies over a skinny latte in Starbucks rather than a darkened office. I always prided myself on learning from experience.

Sitting at my new desk, I heard one officer call Directory Enquiries to ask for a number for the British Embassy in London. Cosmic, I thought.

Every murder is unique, but some more so than others. What follows is one of the most unique cases I was ever involved with.

A teacher had rented a house in west London for several years before one day deciding she would give notice and move on. That done, her landlord popped around one weekend to find reasons to withhold her deposit and found something from a horror film.

A body, bound and gagged, lay decomposing in the garden shed, definitely in breach of contract. It also necessitated a deep clean and they don't come cheap.

This landlord got out of there pretty damn quick, probably gasping and covering his mouth like they do on the telly. Then he called 999 and did battle with the Met Police call handlers and their innate cynicism. 'Please hold the line caller. 'Ere Viv, we got this bloke on line two reckons he's got a dead body in 'is shed.'

'Oh, for fucks sake, don't he know we're chocka until June at the earliest?'

'I hear you, Viv, don't fink that I don't. He's insistent though.'

'I know love. Tell him if he signs up for the premium package today, we'll 'ave two coppers come round and give 'im a quote between 8.00am Monday–11.00pm Friday. Oh, and don't forget the fucking diversity questionnaire before he hangs up will yah?'

Two officers attended to assess the situation. They listened to what the landlord told them and wrote down his name, date of birth and pronouns in their notebooks Then they entered the premises to carry out their sworn duty.

The police have a number of priorities. The first is to ensure their bosses get promoted and don't take the blame for anything. The second is preservation of life. This can involve anything from trying to catch people jumping off buildings to doing that saucy Heimlich manoeuvre on choking grandmothers. Officers are advised to tell members of the public that they are administering urgent first aid when commencing this procedure to avoid being called filthy perverts.

So our two coppers had to go into the house and assess exactly what the score was. It would have been dark and a little bit scary, but that's what we pay their wages for, is it not?

Turned out there was indeed the dead body of someone who'd been tortured which, having had eighteen weeks Police training, enabled them to assess that something had gone badly wrong. Having carried out basic checks for signs of life by shouting, 'are you dead mate?' in the corpse's left then right ear, they followed procedure by searching the rest of the property for extra bodies or suspects who had forgotten to escape. It was completely empty. The teacher had stripped the place of all furniture, but seemed to have overlooked her mutilated victim. 'Keys, wallet, there's something... shit! I'd forget my head if it wasn't screwed on...'

The coppers had no medical training, so had to refer to their find as 'the apparently lifeless body'. One vomited all over it, which isn't standard murder investigation operating procedure, brushed their teeth and helped to set up a Crime Scene.

A police doctor, or Forensic Medical Examiner, was then summonsed who agreed that the tortured corpse was dead. That was all we needed. It was a Sunday and the Murder Squad were on overtime. I was having lunch with my line manager who I also lived with (good for the environment) whe I heard. We deployed with the rest of the so-called Elite Scotland Yard Murder Squad.

The local officers had decided to put on yellow jackets and parade the area conducting 'reassurance patrols'. Each to their own.

We started knocking on doors, putting the frighteners on neighbours who'd no idea a killer had been in their midst and began to lock and bolt doors while making a sign of the cross.

Enquiries revealed that our suspect was a local teacher so we sent the TSG to arrest her, but it turned out she'd recently moved schools. The headmaster told us what he could.

We got the helicopter up to annoy social media commentators and see if our suspect had gone to ground in nearby woodland. It had turned into a full-scale lady hunt. Press Bureau at Scotland Yard had issued the stock lines telling people not to approach the 5ft 2in drama teacher, but to call the police immediately. In case she started doing 'Memories' from *Cats*.

Then our Exhibits Officer arrived, a Detective Constable who spent hours getting into a white suit and hairnet. He finally went into the shed and began the painstaking process of gathering the evidence that might help to convict a serial killer.

Before too long, though, he reappeared with news that made me prematurely stub out a perfectly good cigarette. The body had a label attached: ACME Theatrical Props. It was a dummy from a zombie movie set which, shortly afterwards, took up a position on the local police's senior leadership team.

Missing people often make for the saddest stories.

Charlie grew up in Manchester, in a nice stable home as part of a close-knit family. He did well at school and secured a place at university, the first of them to do so. But unknown to anyone, he had also developed a drinking problem. Rather than face the embarrassment of telling anyone he disappeared, an absence reported to the police who, in those days, did not take reports of missing adults. Every enquiry failed to meet with success. Years later, Charlie's sister married his best friend, the couple staying on in the family home in case Charlie should ever return.

Lila came from Ireland to England to study, the apple of her father's eye. A model student, she excelled academically at a good university. Her dad though had concerns about his daughter. Through her late teens, Lila began to act oddly and it was soon apparent that she was in the early stages of mental illness. Her final descent began at while studying; drug-taking and alcohol abuse speeding her drop-out from uni and return to London.

Lila was still supported by her father but came under the care of mental health services, detained under the Mental Health Act at one point. Upon release, she engaged less and less with support agencies and her drug-taking became worse. Having turned to prostitution to feed her habit, she roamed the capital streets, defying all attempts by nurses and family to make her well again.

One day she met an older man named Charlie, originally from Manchester. He was nice and they'd drink together in his bedsit. He didn't abuse her and so she went there often. They would sometimes row, but there was no violence and the arguing usually descended into a drinking binge. Before long Lila and Charlie were a couple. One night she went to his flat, shown on CCTV entering the block and coming out an hour later. She then tried to sell Charlie's phone to a local shop, went into a phonebox and dialled 999. Charlie was found in his flat, stabbed to death.

Lila was arrested for murder. Her father came to the police station with tears in his eyes, to act as her 'Appropriate Adult' due to her mental health issues. Charlie's family were also traced and a police officer went to see his sister. Twenty-five years after Charlie had disappeared, they had news of him at last.

Lila was charged with murder, however was found unfit to plead. She was detained without limit of time under the Mental

Health Act. Charlie's family attended the hearing and watched as Lila was led away. A sorry tale indeed.

It wasn't long before, under pressure from supervisors and my officers, I opted to leave the Murder Squad. 'You won't be missed,' said my future wife, before giving me the worst Performance Development Review I'd had to that point. And I say that as someone with an earlier appraisal that included the phrase, '...and he was mugged on duty during the period under review.'

While still at Kennington, I'd decided to apply for promotion to prove that the gatekeepers of the High Potential Scheme were mistaken in their assessment that I'd be better off on the bins.

Now, I sat the Inspectors exam with several hundred other Sergeants in a large hall where so many people cheated the test was declared null and void. I found it difficult to accept that police officers would cheat or do anything remotely immoral for personal gain. I had another go and passed. I was going to be a Detective Inspector. People were going to have to call me sir, and not just sarcastic waiters in French restaurants.

As my latest stint in murder spluttered to a halt, I decided to activate the light under my bushel. Which came rather a shock to the cleaner who came into the Gents without knocking.

Making use of my Inspector exam success, I was posted to the London Borough of Ealing and told in no uncertain terms that if I refused the posting I'd be sent there anyway. 'Bet you're fun at parties!' I said to the Postings Panel woman after she hung up. It was the last available posting for newly-minted DIs and I was soon to discover why. Ealing was the worst-performing Borough in the Met. I suppose someone has to come last, as my old PE teacher said to me in the showers after home time once.

Ealing CID was based at Acton. I'd been there years ago with a man I'd kneed in the testicles for trying to stab me in the face. About a year after that I went in there with an Asian colleague, in plain clothes. The Custody Sergeant had assumed he was my prisoner, telling him to shut his fucking mouth and sit on the bench. More recently, rumours of corruption there abounded. Someone on the inside was leaking info to local criminals.

Acton had a reputation – and it wasn't a good one. I should have resigned from the Met right there and then to be honest. But I didn't. Oh, how I would come to regret that!

I got my own desk and computer – exciting times – and shared an office with two other DIs. We would wait for the DCI to leave the building then head to the pub. I later understood that the Detective Sergeants were waiting for us to leave the building before going out to play as well, so the system worked.

Our office was on a corridor shared with senior officers, a right ball ache. I've never got on with seniority, especially the bent ones. I was now, technically, a senior officer too, which fitted my self-hating narrative. One uniformed Superintendent found responsibility a challenge. If asked for his signature on mundane cases he would, without fail, ask you to come back once he'd finished painting his toenails or whatever and then be clocked legging it out the building with a coat over his head.

The next office along was the Detective Chief Inspector, or 'Detective Chief Inspector' as I referred to him with little finger shapes making speech marks in the air. This guy was a career incompetent brought in by the Borough Commander, a very very small man indeed. Both existed purely to win promotion, but strangely never managed to. What. A. Shame. I often thought.

I was put in charge of the Robbery and Burglary Squad, which as I reasoned it meant I was expected to juggle the figures to try and drag Ealing Borough out of the performance quagmire. That was something I wasn't prepared to do, so I found myself on a collision course with the Senior Leadership Team (SLUT). Shit figures do not a promotion make goes the old saying.

Our DCI wore a charity shop Paisley tie of the variety people who don't understand the philosophy of ties wear. He expected me to reach a certain number of detections, he said. This meant making sure someone was charged or cautioned for a certain percentage of reported robberies or residential burglaries. If the detection rates reached a certain level, the Borough would be marked as successful. Ealing was miles off. Things looked grim.

People get charged with crimes when there's enough evidence to satisfy the Crown Prosecution Service. They get cautioned when they admit stuff and agree to have a police Inspector give them a right old telling off. Both outcomes excite senior officers. Having crimes on the books without anyone held to account upsets them. Both are used to compare and contrast senior officers in the race for promotion. Incentive for corruption?

I'd spend most of my time as a DI trying to get my seniors to commit to writing what they expected me to do in terms of crime being detected. They never would, as this was quite obviously cheating. I'd send emails or comments on the Crime Reporting Information System (CHRIST) asking them kindly to advise exactly how they expected me to produce such astonishingly outlandish figures. 'Please speak' they would write, or 'see me', like some rabid schoolmaster. Controversially, I wasn't a fan of getting people to admit to things they hadn't done or making out victims were liars.

As a mild-mannered ginger, I try to love more than fight, but lost my cool once. Having been off sick with righteous anger, on my return I was challenged on what processes I had put in place to have the CID answerphone messages checked within two hours. This was a 'performance indicator'. I threw a pen over the head of the chap doing the asking and things began to seriously disintegrate from there.

Not long after that, I chose to return to uniform duties.

Life's a Riot and Notting Hill Carnival

Having chosen to leave the CID, it was suspected that I was either struggling to cope with my mental health or subject to some sort of ongoing investigation. I'd never sought treatment for my PTSD, it's true, so that could have been the root cause.

I went to see the Chief Inspector in charge of Emergency Response. He was a kind and decent man who did not tread the boards of corruption. I told him I'd like to take the vacant spot for Duty Officer on B Team at Acton. He appeared to be waiting for the punchline, before hitting me with his demand. The door was open, but I'd have to agree to be Public Order trained. This meant wearing all the riot kit and running around shouting and whacking people with long batons.

If there was ever a police officer less suited to Public Order policing than I was, I'd be honoured to meet them. Probably push them around a bit, give them a wedgie maybe. I was a detective born and bred, but needed out of Acton CID. As I left the Chief Inspector's office, I had flashbacks.

I'd been ordered to do basic public order stuff during initial recruit training at Hendon. This stuff took place in Hounslow, west London, chosen for its resemblance to a riot-torn town. Its High Street resembles the bar scene in *Star Wars*.

At training school, I'd already decided my career goal was to be a detective, so spending time in riot uniform while grown men threw rubber bricks at me seemed an irrelevance. If rioting did break out during my career, I intended to be lurking around back street boozers cultivating snouts, not running at people lobbing petrol bombs dressed in an official Met Police romper suit.

My abiding memory of basic public order training was being given a helmet that was too tight, meaning I couldn't hear anything. The visor steamed up as well. This meant that when the Sergeant Major type was bellowing, 'Wheel left' and other ridiculous instructions, I had no idea what was going on. I think he may have used some sweary descriptive terms for me, going by his facial expressions and rude gestures. I couldn't really tell, as my glasses were blurred the whole time.

I went to east London for a full uniform fitting. This was done in a secret police location because they also stored lots of seized money and drugs there. Many bent detectives went to get kitted out having been busted back to uniform. This was seen as a punishment to avoid the unpleasantness of formal disciplinary action. I think the cash and gear was kept in the same place to taunt them. I made it quite clear to the tailors that I was not a bent cop and had chosen a return to uniform of my own volition, but I think they'd heard it all before. I noticed they checked they still had their wallets after coming close to me to measure what side I dressed on.

I was sent to a new Public Order Centre in Gravesend, which

is in Kent's patch, but their cahoonas weren't big enough to tell the Met to piss off. Aside from public order, the centre was also used for firearms training and offered respite care for uniformed psychopaths. We were expected to spend two days role playing scenarios, at the conclusion of which we would be qualified Level 2 Public Order officers. Level 3 is lowest level, awarded to people who can read and write. Level 1 is for those who breathe through their mouths. Level 2 is the Liberal Democrats equivalent.

I was given full riot kit, which I never managed to master. Too many pads and straps. I did get to wear special red epaulets 'cos I was a proper important Inspector. And the helmet fitted properly this time. I was in charge of a Police Support Unit (PISS) made up of three Sergeants and a smattering of Constables. They all got to dress up as well, but nothing in red for them. Public order policing boiled down to the PCs all standing in a line, with the Sergeants standing behind them to stop them running away or fainting. My role was to keep well out of the way and not to interfere with people who knew what they were doing. As any decent senior police officer should do.

The first test was a pass or fail shield run. We all put our PE kit on and picked up a long shield. This is a shield that is longer than a short shield which is shorter than a long shield. We then had to run at full pelt until one of the shouty instructor men screamed at you to stop. If you couldn't complete the shield run you had to go and sit on the coach until everyone else was ready to go home.

It was a tough run, but I managed it despite being a massive fan of fags and booze. The embryonic cord of the CID is a hard one to cut. The shield run was banned a few years later because someone felt upset by it and said they might think about going to an Employment Tribunal once they'd had a nice lie down.

After I'd asked a somewhat surprised PC to help me get dressed in my riot gear, we all went for a warm-up. The shouty men made us prance around in circles and shout abuse at the

Kent officers, who watched us through binoculars from the other side of the demarcation line.

We were then called meaningless pieces of shite and had the backs of our heads slapped. After which they called forward all the people who had never been to Level 2 public order training before. A few PCs stepped forwards, but I held firm. I was an Inspector. Some twat pushed me from behind, and the shouty people got very excited, like the monkeys at the start of *2001: A Space Odyssey*. It wasn't often they had a newbie of rank.

We were sprayed with petrol and set on fire for the baying entertainment of the seasoned riot pros. It proved our kit was flameproof. This was of little consolation to the passing CID officer who went up like a rocket. I imagined the alcohol fumes acted as an accelerant.

After I'd been hosed down, we were given a shouted briefing about our first exercise. We were to escort some pretend football hooligans from a pretend train station to an imaginary football match. We'd 'bubble' them, which was like a cuddling game for grown-ups. The hooligans were officers who got to chant 'BNP! BNP!' in work time without attracting the attention of the press.

Next up was an angry person upstairs in a pretend house. This would be one of the shouty men dressed up in a padded outfit called a 'fister suit'. We used shields to pin him in a corner and drag him underneath before sitting on him until he said 'sorry' and 'pretty please'. As an Inspector, I got to offer barbed criticisms of the Sergeants who would pass on my thoughts to the PCs by banging their helmets together. It was never explained exactly what the fister had done to cause a riot squad to smash him up; I don't think the shouty men bothered about law and procedure too much. I asked one what act and section we were using, but he just dribbled.

The evening exercise loomed. We would, along with other trainees, deal with an ever-worsening riot. The shouty men and their fat mates from the golf club would throw petrol bombs at us. We were to be assessed on our ability to use increasing levels of force to control them. The first level was standing there with moody facial expressions. If that didn't work, we would move up to verbal commands such as, 'Leave it out! It ain't worth it!' And if that didn't work, I would be expected to read the Riot Act as the Inspector. I used a loudhailer: 'You treat this place like a hotel. If you don't get a job and start paying your way, you'll have to go and live with your father and that slag Hilda!'

A police dog would then go nuts for a bit, before being let loose on the bloke with the padded arm who always turns up at riots and village fêtes. If the mentalist German Shepherds didn't stop the rioters, I would be allowed to decide to ask the police horses if they wouldn't mind popping along.

I left the PCs playing keepie-up with petrol bombs and nipped around the corner. There was a load of police horses with coppers on them, so I asked if they'd seen Mounted Branch. I was directed to a Chief Inspector. She had really super orange epaulettes. I told ma'am that there was a bally riot going on. I asked that the horses walk around the corner and stand behind our lines so the rioters could see them. The idea was that they'd bottle it, and make some excuses about needing an early night. I then returned to my chaps and helped the larger one put his boots on the right feet. I stood the Sergeants in height order and waited for the gentle clip clop of equestrian feds. Then I turned around.

I was faced with a full battalion of riot horses charging at us at full pelt. The Chief Inspector had misheard my briefing and interpreted 'walk peacefully and stop' as 'FUCKING CHARGE THE BASTARDS!' I screamed at my officers to dive out the way and legged it. The nags thundered between us. The rioters were equally surprised and used a lot of swear words in the debrief afterwards. I just kept saying, 'Well, did it stop the riot or not?' which won the day. In my mind.

I was a Level 2 Public Order trained Inspector! Good god, the Met were desperate.

My first public order duty was Notting Hill Carnival. Several thousand public order officers are required to police this event every year. I like NHC. There. I've said it.

The early shifts saw the true spirit of Carnival, people for whom the event and location had a deep meaning. The stall holders, the Rastafarians, organisers. They were all fascinating to talk to and reminded me that being a police officer would find you engaged in conversation with a far wider spectrum of humanity than I'd otherwise have experienced over my garden wall in Wellingborough, Northamptonshire. I was never called a ginger four eyes policing Notting Hill Carnival. Well, hardly ever.

It's bloody loud, though. And don't believe the crime figures either.

The public order stuff comes later in the day when all the gang chaps have got out of bed and had a hearty breakfast. My first public order aid saw me with a crew of Level 2 officers on the parade route. For the first half, we would patrol around, squeezing through the massed crowds, feeling the tensions in the air get harsher with time and masses of alcohol and pungent self-rolled cigarettes. The smell of those certainly helped me relax.

We were instructed to keep a low profile, not antagonise the gangsta community all around us. Senior officers simply love to declare each year a Carnival success. This is not the experience of the public order officers on the ground. But who cares about their views? I, for one, fucking do not.

Our sector big boss, a Superintendent, made it quite clear this was his last Carnival and that he didn't want trouble. The ink was still drying on his promotion application and managing a successful Carnival sector was big Brownie points.

All of a sudden, we came across two gangs fighting each other. We managed to force them in separate directions, encouraging them to go and get an ice cream. Making arrests in the Carnival footprint is heavily discouraged. It upsets the senior officer whose turn it is to talk unfiltered bollocks on the local TV news.

Anyway, we carried on waddling around and suddenly were surrounded by one of the gangs. Not one of them had a Cornetto. We'd been tricked and now were trapped: chaos.

We came under a relentless hail of bottles as the crowd scattered. As bottles arced through the sky, I ordered my officers to do some public order. We were being attacked from all sides. The passing parade stopped. One MC had turned off his music, demanding the gang stop attacking the police using rhyming couplets. I'd like to take this opportunity to thank him, and to request 'Summer Holiday' by Cliff Richard for Doreen in Littlehampton, who is 76 today.

I directed my team to put on their riot helmets. The bottles were coming thick and fast and I had genuine fears for our safety. Some were full-sized brandy jobs that could fracture a skull as easily as falling over in a petrol station. Suddenly I heard bellowing in my ear. It was our boss. I was impressed. He'd come to help his staff who were under sustained attack in a pre-planned ambush.

No, he hadn't. Promotion was disappearing before his eyes.

'Get those fucking helmets off now!' he screamed.

'These are known gang members throwing bottles at my officers,' I retorted.

'Get those fucking helmets off now! You are antagonising the community!' he countered.

I ignored him, more interested in stopping my officers being hospitalised. He scuttled away and I never heard anything about it again. I had directly refused an order as well. Crazy times.

The whole incident was captured on CCTV. I assumed, in my naivety, that my team and I would be contacted to provide statements, that our attack would be vigorously investigated, that the gang members would be brought to justice. Nothing ever happened. Weird that.

I bet our Superintendent got promoted though.

Some big wig or other from Beijing was in London. We police were posted outside the Chinese Embassy to control protesters cordoned opposite, and briefed that someone lobbed an egg the day before. China had got really cross and told Britain it couldn't come to the President's birthday party if it happened again.

Either that or something about no longer investing billions of pounds in mobile phone technology to control our brains. My attention span is woefully short during briefings.

Close to one hundred riot trained officers were mustered to prevent anyone else upsetting the People's Republic, all taken from local Borough duties, which meant a hundred fewer officers to deal with 999 calls. Oh, well. As long as some VIP communist didn't get yolk in his hair weave.

There were three protesters. One was dressed as a panda – the focus of a massive operation. 'Watch his hands! Watch his hands!' bellowed our boss every time it scratched its arse.

Not long after this intelligent use of tax payers money, we were out in force yet again – this time to face: Students!

The government had told a lie and the students waved their skinny little fists in the air and promised revolution, with trigger warnings. Finding out that politicians lie felt like learning about Santa. I was twenty-two years old when that happened to me and it still gives me the shakes.

The students put on a big march through central London, so the university of life graduates could slag them off in poorly gramatically rants on social media. End off.

I was in charge of leading the march to the agreed musterpoint where they'd hear speeches from people with patches on their jacket elbows. I clarified that I was a police officer and not representing the Open University, although I *was* doing a life drawing class at the time, so felt a little conflicted. The briefing Superintendent just looked at me. I bet he'd have loved to have slapped the back of my head so my glasses fell off. Education triggers coppers.

The crowd was a merry old bunch and we chatted happily as we awaited lift-off. Middle-aged men who lived in their mother's basements gave out revolutionary leaflets, communicating with each other via Vulcan hand signals. They would steadfastly refuse to speak to police officers, maintaining their radical stance by saying 'Pigs' behind our backs before pretending they were coughing when we turned round.

The march set off and, SHOCK HORROR, they decided to stop in front of the Houses of Parliament to shout at the MPs wallowing around in the subsidised bars behind legions of police officers and metal barriers. I was ordered to move the march along but they all sat on the floor, as students do. One got on top of a portable toilet and set fire to it. Direct action against shitting. Yeah! Smash the state!

They sent TSG to replace us in multi-coloured riot helmets. The Inspectors wore red, resembling an inflamed penis. I suspect word had got around that I was an OU student, so they worried I might defect. As time wore on, someone really really clever and important decided we would clear Parliament Square by making sure nobody could leave it for the next few hours. This technique became known as kettling. It was intended to contain the trouble makers, who couldn't go off and bring down capitalism by spray painting penises on McDonald's windows.

So the streets were closed and we stood there. For hours. And hours. Some students sang 'Silent Night' to us, which was nice. It stopped what was left of my brain going into hibernation.

The next big decision was to move all the remaining students onto Westminster Bridge and make them stand there for even more hours. The TSG did that, penis helmets leading from the front. My serial were ordered to run down to the next bridge, then back along the south side of the River Thames to assist in closing Westminster Bridge from the other side. This was bloody knackering in full riot kit. Some lah-di-da serials did it with military precision. We were like the muppets on roller skates. To this day, I have no idea what the thinking behind shoving them all onto the bridge, then keeping them there for another few hours, was. All the trouble makers had gone, and by that time of night were being tucked in by nanny.

I had a little lie down on a pavement.

Taken into Custody and Outdoor Rumpy-Pumpy

Back in the real world, I was once again a uniformed Duty Officer. The Inspector in charge of a team of officers dedicated to dealing with emergencies across my patch of west London. Acton and Ealing were my domain. Southall was covered by another Inspector who spent his time sleeping in the locker room prior to retirement. He'd been asked to leave the armed policing command. I never asked why in case he pistol-whipped me.

A key role was taking command of spontaneous incidents. Proper grown up stuff at last. I spent a lot of my time as a Detective Inspector avoiding the DCI by hiding in a cupboard with other pungent men when we heard him thundering down the corridor. I'd also been formally disciplined for sitting in an aggressive manner while being threatened by a member of police staff. One of my more unusual disciplinary findings. As a Duty Inspector, the buck well and truly stopped with me. I'd have to learn to control my sitting aggression and act like a real grown up boy. Bugger.

Shakespeare described uniformed response work thus: 'The policeman who lashes the whore has a hot need to use her for the very offense for which he plies the lash.' No, me neither. The drudgery of shift work, coupled with the most base of engagement with the public at large, is seen as beyond the pale for the ambitious leaders of tomorrow. Those seeking the kudos of detective squads or a fast track to senior management escape the witch's claw of response work at the earliest opportunity.

Traditionally, all police officers were expected to serve their first two years on emergency response. For those of a more sensitive disposition, it can make or break you. No matter your previous life experience, relentless 999 work is destructive, both physically and mentally. Some find it isn't for them and leave to seek fame and fortune in more gentle surroundings. Others keep their head down and wait for the chance to retreat. Very few find their whole careers stretch across it. Not many return from CID.

When I started as a Duty Officer, the police were meant to turn up to emergencies within twelve minutes. When austerity started to bite and some pulsating bell end at the Home Office coined the phrase 'more for less', attendance time was raised to fifteen minutes. It was the Duty Officer's responsibility to ensure that time was met. If missed, the Duty Officer would be tarred, feathered and dragged around the yard for the pleasure of the Senior Leadership Team (TITS).

Senior Leaders created league tables, showing each of the five response teams in various lights. If a Duty Officer failed to meet the charter time for a call, their name would be highlighted in CAPITALS by the Chief Inspector and they would be ordered to justify their failures before a baying audience of their peers. The obvious response, 'give me more officers, police cars and a sense of destiny and I'll meet all your targets you promotion hungry chopper' was unacceptable. If the call is not an emergency, you'll get police within the hour. Yeah. Whatever.

I also had Custody Suite responsibilities. As Duty Inspector, I had to make sure the arrested felt well cared for following arrest.

Some years ago, you would be chucked in a cell and left there until you'd admitted to a number of burglaries. Sometimes you were assisted in your decision making by visits from the more muscular members of the CID. You'd also be asked to grass up others. I found this area to be a double-edged sword. Cough.

By the time I became a uniformed Inspector, newly arrested persons got to spend the first two hours answering welfare questions. What is the likelihood of killing yourself, on a scale of one to ten? Are you allergic to anything apart from the arresting officer? Would you like a salad? Detainees were asked if they'd like to make a call, but not to the person they'd just battered or Bent Benny who owed them a fucking score. Finally, the suspect was offered free and independent legal advice (in the form of the sixth former from a law firm over the road most likely).

The booking-in procedure could be delayed if the arrested person was carried in upside down by the officers they'd been fighting for the last hour. In such cases, the subject was 'placed' in a cell and left until they stopped throwing a tantrum and developed a civil tongue in their head.

Then they got to say sorry to the Custody Sergeant and to make formal complaints of assault against the arresting officers. If the chap couldn't calm himself, a couple of police officers sat and stared at him. This is called a 'constant watch' and means exactly that. Even when taking a poo.

As the Custody Inspector, I was required to review such detentions. I'd have to speak to them, make sure they were fully aware of their rights. Under no circumstances whatsoever could I advise them that if they hadn't broken the law they wouldn't be here in the fucking first place.

I reviewed a celebrity once. It's to my lasting shame I didn't manage to incorporate his catchphrase into his detention review. I did tell him he was much smaller than he was on telly though.

When I was at Shepherd's Bush, some bloke who'd been on a soap opera was arrested for wife-beating. Some of the officers on duty took to whistling its theme tune outside his cell. This really upset him. He tried to kick the cell door off in his espadrilles.

Once I escaped from Custody, I was put in charge of policing the mean streets. Having been away from frontline uniformed policing for many years, it felt like I was getting back to basics. Squaring things away seemed consigned to the past. Despite my best efforts to re-introduce Shepherd's Bush methods, the young officers under my command were strangely reticent. They drank a lot less as well. I'm pretty sure the two issues were connected.

As the Duty Officer, I was responsible for everything. It really is amazing that the times of highest demand seem adversely to coincide with the absence of senior officers. I was always reliant on my team Sergeants to show me what to do and to keep the PCs under control. I started off with the 'my door is always open' nonsense, but reversed this after a young officer came to me for relationship advice when her boyfriend left. 'Like men, all coppers are bastards,' I said, gently escorting her from the room.

My first two Sergeants supported me through my CID withdrawal. One was a German tank commander in a previous life and still struggled with the outcome of 1945. The other should have been on a register. They would take turns at being Custody Sergeant or going out on patrol, driving me around. One of them nearly killed me once, hitting a kerb at high speed and causing our car to skid across Uxbridge Road, one of the busiest routes in west London. After the car finished pulling donuts, he made me promise never to tell anyone what happened, a promise I intend to keep.

Aside from emergency calls and custody issues, Duty Officers are also expected to command spontaneous firearms incidents, i.e. the ones that take the police by surprise, i.e. the vast majority unless the Duty Officer is psychic. I've often used the phrase, 'Because I don't have a fucking crystal ball, guv.' Never worked.

I was sent back to the training centre in Gravesend to learn how to tell armed police what to do. I hadn't mastered the art of taking the free cab service from the station to the training centre, so walked through the pouring rain. I arrived in my re-born CID suit soaking wet, so got off to a good start.

We were instructed to manage an interactive filmed scenario that involved a child being taken hostage in a house. The roughty toughty firearms cops would come and shout at you, demanding you give them direction. I agreed that a sniper would blow the chap's head off to save the child. I screamed and fell to the floor sobbing, before the instructor convinced me it was make believe. I didn't really have the blood of an innocent on my hands. He couldn't convince me *ET* was just a film though. Nobody can.

I managed to pass, but the certificate was ruined by rain on my walk back to the station. Luckily, my online personel file now included authority to order people with guns around in a spontaneous way and I returned to Acton with a god complex and Tactical Firearms Commander underpants.

If someone called and mentioned shooters, I would make the initial assessment. This basically meant deciding if it was going to be run as a firearms incident or not. If it was, I'd get at least three carloads of heavily armed cops. If no, I'd send a probationer in, just in case. Last in first out. In a coffin or otherwise.

After my decision, I'd have a few minutes to phone a tactical advisor (an expert in shooting stuff, who sat in a Lambeth control room). They would call me sir, but wouldn't mean it, and offer tactical options before making a recommendation. Disagreeing with that meant you were a proper bell-end.

The role of Duty Officers in running firearms calls would be withdrawn some months after I did the course because of an excess of proper bell-ends.

One area of west London was well known for outdoor rumpy-pumpy. The Met decided such areas be officially known as Public Sex Environments (PEE), chiefly parks, public toilets and phone boxes. The policy was written by officers who had no personal interest in such activities whatsoever, so help them God.

One fateful night, we had a number of reports of members of the travelling community arriving to set up home in their caravans amongst the hedge shaggers. Convention dictated that we would send a probationer to ask them what they were up to, and tell them to move on. If they declined to move on, we would withdraw and attend the following day to tell them to move on. This process would be repeated ad-infinitum. On this occasion, I assumed that there was a senior police officer on scene getting rogered in the bushes, so left it to their discretion.

One of the travellers had found himself in a bit of bother with another travelling gentleman. He felt that the dispute might end with his protagonist turning up with a shotgun. He was a little on edge as he set up home in Lovers Lane. A few hours after arriving, he called 999, insisting his life was in danger from a car outside, whose driver had a long-barrelled weapon in his lap. He was sure the bloke was armed and he also had a female passenger whose head he was pushing down presumably to avoid detection.

By this time, Duty Officers weren't allowed to do firearms incidents anymore, so the joy of local knowledge was gone. A Tactical Firearms Commander elsewhere in London would run the show. The armed units were organised from central London.

An update came through that the weapon was still in the suspect's lap, who was now backing towards the car park exit and still had the woman in his vehicle. Who was she? Was this guy there to kill the traveller, or was it just a warning? I imagine the Firearms Inspector had all those thoughts. I know I did.

His troops were now getting properly excited – their voices husky on the radio – at the idea of doing a 'hard stop', which is basically smashing shit up and dragging people through car windows by their hair, while shouting swear words in gas masks.

Even though I was getting quite pumped myself, I thought it only right to let the Inspector know the area was a Public Sex Environment and his officers might encounter local dignitaries at the scene. He thanked me for my concern and carefully wrote down the address and directions from the A40.

So the hard stop went in as planned and a half-dressed chap with an extended organ was forcibly removed from the vehicle. His shame-faced girlfriend explained that they'd gone to the area for an amorous outing, but had been somewhat discouraged by a traveller screaming something about not shooting him and how sorry he was about disrespecting the driver's mother.

It really was amazing what went down sometimes.

And so to a night shift known to those in the know as Fireworks Night. A rather lame title for what follows if I may be so honest.

My shift predecessor had dealt with an incident on the East Acton Estate. A shotgun had been fired through a young gent's front door. As is common with people who get shot at, he had simply been minding his own business with no idea why anyone would want to get trigger happy in his direction. He would, however, be sorting matters out himself and did not require the assistance of the Constabulary. I had flashbacks to that long-ago time when knee met nuts, nostalgia a strange mistress.

The scene of the shooting was being treated as a crime scene, as hardworking taxpayers would expect. Due to the time of night, the CID were down the pub, meaning uniformed officers had to stand outside the house for the rest of the evening. It was decided that to deploy armed officers for this would involve far too much paperwork, so we defaulted to using a probationer with a small can of CS spray and a winning smile. Should the gunman return, they were briefed to fucking leg it over the back gardens.

By this time in my ever faltering career, I'd had a Sergeant change, which is like an oil change but with a different dipstick. I had less than satisfactory replacements angling for my attention like labradors on heat. Two were particularly keen on a higher rank, one of whom offered to visit the scene and gauge the risk. Upon arrival, he got a feel for it straight away. A car was being driven at high speed towards the address. Suspecting it might be armed gunmen returning for a second go, he stepped into the roadway and indicated for the vehicle to stop, using Met Police approved hand signals. The car though accelerated, causing our chap to lumber out of the way, missed by inches. His breathless transmission over the police radio left us in stitches.

As the boss man, I recognised that I'd have to go to the scene and take command of what might have been attempted murder. I was driven there by underling two, in his over-tight uniform.

As we arrived, our man was flailing around on the pavement, gesturing up the road. The car that tried to run him down was still there! They'd come back for a second pop. My driver put on the nee-naw sounds and we had a car chase. The radio controller kept saying the pursuit wasn't authorised, but I was the Duty Officer and did what the fuck I wanted. The offending vehicle ended up down a cul-de-sac and its driver legged it. My officer got out and gave chase but suddenly the engine of the car we'd been following started up again. The passenger had leapt across into the driving seat and was now trying to escape me. I recall thinking that there was no respect for authority anymore.

At the wheel was a woman who looked as if she was dressed for church. She tried to drive off, so I smashed the window with my extendable baton, which made a right mess. Then she leapt out of the car and started fighting with me, which I didn't really expect a woman of such sober appearance to do.

Her shouting and shrieking drew attention to her plight and I was soon surrounded by concerned locals, who believed they had found the feds beating up an innocent young lady in their road. I didn't mention she'd tried to kill one of our officers in case they'd met him and would then naturally side with her. As they grew more hostile and seemed about to rescue the churchgoer, I yelled, 'She's just shot someone! It could have been any one of you!' and they all cleared off, so I could arrest her in peace.

A few streets away, my colleague's chase ended when a police dog indicated the suspect lying under a car with a nice big bag of cannabis. 'I've been out for a jog and am having a lie-down!' he insisted. 'Woof!' laughed the dog. And then it all went tits up.

I ordered some of our minions to come and escort us and our prisoners back to Acton Police Station. Going through a Sun God phase, I demanded they never look me directly in the eye. While one helped his prisoner have a natural, I stepped into the yard. It was a fresh, balmy evening and I'd earned my Queen's shilling. We'd caught the people who'd tried to run a policeman down. It was lucky we identified them so quickly because the list of people willing to run that particular one down was substantial.

The Duty Officer's phone rang. Never a good sign. A PC was rattling on about something not looking good. I did my usual gag of suggesting he see a doctor. As he was in conversation with a senior officer, it wasn't appropriate for him to tell me to fuck off, so we had a moments respectful silence before he continued.

It turned out that some nosey parker had called 999 after a birthday party in a restaurant in West Ealing went beyond the negative review on Trip Advisor stage. It became apparent that a gang-banger* was celebrating his special day with gang-banging friends. A resident of a neighbouring Borough, said gang-banger

---

* *The terms 'gang banger' and 'gang banging' may be of interest to the reader in a strictly professional capacity. The author strongly advises against researching said terms on work IT systems. He was once encouraged by colleagues to research 'scat lover' on the Met's internet server. His eyes remain bleached by the experience.*

had been surprised that his dear old mum had booked a place in what turned out to be rival gang-banging territory.

As is their wont, several hostile gang members started to prowl around doing that hard gangster walk where you drag one leg behind the other with the back of your jeans lowered. My darling officers felt concerned enough about this to call their lord and master. As I was doing my best to end the call, the PC began to shout about people shooting each other and lost his shit. The control room leapt into action and called me on the radio. I answered in a disinterested way to make sure they knew who the boss was. I needed to get to the scene and do some commanding.

The only copper available to drive me over to West Ealing was the one who'd nearly been run over. A bit worrying that. Other people might be out to get him and I didn't want to get hit by shrapnel having just had my hair done. As he drove really fast along Uxbridge Road I ate palmfuls of Jelly Babies, proper hyper by the time we arrived. There were people running everywhere, shouting and screaming. Bedlam. I got out of the car and pushed my hat back in a way intended to dominate proceedings.

Some Southall officers had turned up at the west side of the disturbance, which showed how serious things were becoming. They were led by a Sergeant who, acting tough, dismissively made out that Acton coppers were sissies. Another report came over the radio of shots being fired, which this Sergeant smugly made out to be fireworks. One Acton PC splendidly noted that a bullet had in fact struck the floor by his feet as he was milling with some ruffians. 'Touché!' I noted, asking for my comments to be noted on the rolling computer log by the control room. Don't forget the accute accent aboue the é, I stressed.

The radio then lit up with officers talking about being shot at and chasing people armed with axes. A paramedic who had been parked nearby to catch up on paperwork called in to say he'd seen a man with a gun run into the side of his ambulance. Brilliant!

We needed strategic action. My driver was chasing a group of gang bangers into a hotel before I stopped him and ordered all unarmed officers to withdraw to the RVP, re-enforcing this by saying 'fucking' over the radio like a proper boss man. One area car took this so seriously they nearly ran me over. It's possible they were aiming for my colleague, there being a lot of that about.

Another officer, desperate to get a bravery commendation, disobeyed and carried on fighting. I think his fiancée had made that a condition of accepting his proposal. I'd have said the f word again, but knew some of the radio operators were a tad sensitive. I'd called one of them an arse hat once and they'd gone sick.

Even the Fire Brigade got involved. As they had a Christmas do in a pub, a gang banger was set upon outside and had acid thrown in his face. Gross. In the finest traditions of pissed emergency service workers the length and breadth of the British Isles, they legged it outside for a punch up and saved his life.

I demanded armed backup but got a Superintendent for some reason. He just stood watching. I asked for *quelle surprise* to be added to the rolling computer record by the arse hats, but they wrote *quiche Lorraine* in a deliberate attempt to undermine my authority and draw ridicule in the later debrief.

Some armed fellas finally turned up and I made out like some war veteran welcoming fresh meat to the 'Nam. Like in *Platoon*. I asked for the Commissioners Reserve, not a reference to the top cop's innate shyness but a group of TSG officers on duty with the sole purpose of going to the area of London where most trouble could be caused as quickly as possible in riot clothes.

They duly turned up and arrested some bloke for using a stolen credit card in a strip club. This had nothing to do with the armed incident, but TSG officers are entranced by strip clubs. The whole lot of them then cleared off to book the prisoner in and drink the fake champagne they'd paid over £200 a bottle for. Useless tossers. As I noted on the computer record.

The dust finally settled in the early hours and I had a massive crime scene covering one of the main routes through west

London. I took great pleasure in closing it, leaving a requirement for seventeen officers to stand guard for the incoming Inspector. He said, 'How many?' like a really angry cartoon headmaster, as I legged it out the back gate.

Coming to work the next night I learned one gunman had travelled over on the bus. He'd used his Oyster card to tap in, so the detectives didn't have their work cut out but still claimed they had. He was on CCTV getting off the bus with a gun in his hand. I hope he thanked the driver.

I remembered I'd left my prisoner behind when going off to West Ealing. Turned out she sat on a bench in the custody suite for hours until one Sergeant asked her what she was doing. She said, 'The policeman said I'd shot someone, but I never mister.' So they let her out. I was grateful. It saved a ton of paperwork.

Being a Duty Officer was very much about learning as you go along/making shit up. Every incident was dealt with by some very committed police. And me.

Taking command also meant imagining worst-case scenarios, and how I'd justify my actions to the Senior Leadership Team at Operation Hindsight meetings. It wasn't called morning prayers anymore since the wrath of God was visited on Scotland Yard via a plague of locusts in the ACPO soft play area.

Emergency response police work is notoriously unpredictable and ruins many a good SLT performance indicator. They still had them mind. No matter what serious incidents you safely resolved, the SLT would want to know why you failed in some pointless objective about paperclips or oven chips. As a matter of principle, I remained committed to not checking answerphone recordings.

The Senior Leadership Team changed around this time and the new boss was a nice bloke who obsessed about how many police officers were in each police car at any one time. He'd sit by his window in Ealing police station waiting for one to go past. If there was more than one PC inside, he'd call the Duty Officer and ask difficult questions. I used to answer in a funny accent and pretend he'd got the wrong number, but he wasn't fooled.

The officers were supposed to patrol on their own so we could all pretend that austerity hadn't made any difference to police resilience. Response teams were significantly reduced. The only department in the Met that didn't suffer a reduction in numbers was the office who decided where the cuts were going to be made. Anyway, the boss's difficult questions ended when he got arrested and then sacked for leaking confidential information to a journalist while on the Murder Squad. Borough Commanders were dropping like flies! Things can only get better I thought, like the naïve bell-end I was in those days.

On night shifts, we were free of line management interference so entertained ourselves, often with discounted refreshments. We would go to a petrol station in Acton who offered free hot drinks to the emergency services, but charged the AA double.

I often stood around drinking coffee with Sergeants while PCs did the police work. Sometimes Chiswick officers nipped across the border to nab cheap coffee, but we'd chase them with brooms. The Acton garage was our domain and one we guarded jealously.

A staff member there was Polish and took every opportunity to improve his English. Someone had told him the English for chocolate sprinkles was 'jizz'. So one fine night, he asked a police officer if he wanted jizz on his cappuccino. My god, dear reader, I nearly died. I still won't have chocolate on coffee to this day.

By the way, that staff member was later arrested for assaulting a co-worker. I've always wondered if the events were connected.

Worst Case Scenarios and a Pit of Despair

Writing about police work is very difficult without the shadow of death falling across everything. The Murder Squad was good for turning up mob-handed in sharp suits to deal with suspicious fallouts. Reactive investigations have strict guidelines to ensure the best evidence is gathered and, more importantly, to prevent the Met getting hauled across the coals at a public enquiry. Again.

Emergency response is the world of the unknown. What an officer on the ground is given seconds to decide can often be subject to years of criticism by those in expensive shoes and nice offices with vegan sandwich delivery.

At training school, our attention was drawn to a declaration printed in the back of the police notebook. This was to be written prior to a record being made of the last words of a dying person.

It is held in law that a person in hopeless expectation of death can tell no lies. Therefore, should the name of the killer be disclosed to the police officer cradling their head, it can be submitted in evidence.

I have a name in mind should I ever find myself in such a situation, whether they did it or not. James Myers. He stuck his tongue out at me on my first day at school and I've never gotten over it. His name shall be on my lips as my soul departs.

The first objective of the police is the preservation of life. Officially. Unofficially, it's the preservation of their corporate reputation, but I digress. If a 999 call directs officers to a life-threatening situation, they are duty-bound to make every effort to prevent death. Police officers do the most heroic acts to save people. All the time. Officers are supposed to complete mental dynamic risk assessments before acting. This means imaging the worst-case scenario and reasoning whether better trained or equipped officers would be best suited to resolving the incident.

As the Duty Officer, I would often find that, in practice, this meant officers diving in headfirst like utter throbbers. I grew tired of the number of times I'd attend an incident only to find myself demanding officers get out of rivers, get down from high roofs, or not tackle knife-wielding lunatics with witty bantz.

If it's all too late and someone dies, dear old Scotland Yard gets involved and wants to know if the corpse had any previous dealings with the police. This is so some poor unfortunate can be hung out to dry after several years of investigation. It is right that the police are held to account, but it would be really nice if such investigations took account of the workloads of the officer concerned, the resources allocated to support them by senior officers, and the sustainability of the policies and procedures they are governed by. But that's not going to happen.

As a Duty Officer, I would often have to attend scenes of death to decide if it was in any way suspicious. If not, the body would be taken away by the undertakers, and a lone PC would be left to complete cursory paperwork. If suspicious, a crime scene was put in place and a major investigation launched.

A murder enquiry can offer answers. If someone has been murdered, there will be someone to blame. If a death is non-suspicious, a different process takes place. The Coroner decides who someone was and how they died. *Who someone was.* A tragedy of society is the number of people who lie dead in the streets and houses all around us for weeks or months on end. A stench from the letterbox, an unpaid bill. A human being whose absence from society is only noticed when they decompose.

It was a morning of such crisp freshness. The sun came out early and the birds celebrated in trees lining a comfortable area of Ealing. The air cleared your lungs and promised good health.

The dwelling was one you couldn't mistake for one anywhere other than in a London suburb. Notionally detached, it offered a sliver of space between each house, just enough for the rising sun to glare through and light the delicate plants potted across the terracotta paving leading up to the front door.

The avenue slept in a stillness broken only by a jet climbing out of Heathrow. An ambulance and panda car, not quite parked straight, waited outside. Porch door open, the inside was dark.

Voices came from the kitchen, low, careful, professional. The ambulance crew, paperwork, a PC by the door in the shadows. Her flatmates were there as well. It was they who had found her.

The garden was a long one, trellis fencing down each side overlooking pampered flowerbeds interspersed with small trees. She had hung herself from one of those, off a stool carried from the kitchen, rope looped over a branch, put around her neck, and then she'd dropped. Twenty-three years old.

Another evening saw a Social Worker call us for assistance to place a young man into the formal care of the Mental Health Services, via a Court Order. The official procedure was that he would be taken in an ambulance to a mental health facility where a bed was waiting for him to receive the treatment he needed.

If there is a potential risk to the safety of the Social Worker or ambulance crew, police officers may attend to assist. As it is a medical matter, the police can't take the lead role. Having mental health issues is not criminal. The ambulance service, stretched as ever, were unable to get there for several hours, so I directed my two officers to withdraw as well, and arrangements were left to the Social Worker. And then the young man hung himself.

I, along with social services and a representative of the London Ambulance Service were called to Coroners Court to assist. His death was deemed a suicide, but one that may not have happened had public services not been at breaking point. We had all followed policy and procedure but it felt so desperately wrong and sad that someone in such desperate need of help could die.

Such tragedies are all around. The people in all the services mentioned still feel a desperate sense of shame and loss, but are hamstrung by a fatal lack of resources.

One day the cities of England fell to rioting. An armed operation in the Met had led to the death of a man from Tottenham. The rioting tore across London, then spread to other urban centres.

On the night Ealing exploded, my team was on night duty. Ealing, that most genteel place of black and white comedies with its ancient common. A place of wealth and calm besmirched as hooded and masked youths looted and destroyed over three lawless nights of darkness.

Police support for areas under attack was very limited in the first outbreaks. My officers, regular response PCs, were forced to defend Ealing against a mob hellbent on destruction. They saw an innocent man punched to the ground by a rioter, but were unable to go to his assistance due to the large, hostile crowds all around them. The man would die of his injuries. His killer would be convicted of his manslaughter and his mother of attempting to pervert the course of justice, having assisted in disposing of the clothing he'd worn at the time he killed a man.

I missed the first nights of rioting, on holiday in Wales. The officer who covered for me remains unspeakably angry about this. To this day.

Just west of Ealing lies Southall. Southall was originally a Welsh community, so you will note how I've cleverly managed to link my choice of holiday destination with the worst outbreak of rioting on the British mainland since the early 1980s.

Southall is now known as the mini Punjab. It contains many places of religious worship. The oldest Hindu Temple sits on King Street, with the largest Sikh Gurdwara outside India just around the corner in Havelock Road. During the rioting, police units attempted to disperse crowds away from Ealing Broadway by pushing them towards Southall. And the people of Southall and friends and family from further afield descended on the area to protect their homes and places of worship from the lawless rioters coming from the east.

Reports were made of burly men armed with large swords patrolling the area, offering severe repercussions to anyone who dared cross into their territory. And word spread somehow to the rioters who pleaded with officers to arrest them rather than cause them to face the wrath of Southall. The place remained free of disorder for the duration. When a local community comes together, it is indeed a joy to behold.

Police Supports Units were sent from all over the country to control areas ravaged by it all. I'd been forced to come back to work as, apparently, it was my job. We'd be on twelve-hour shifts for the foreseeable future, so many officers got all dramatic and slept in corridors. As Duty Officer, I was responsible for directing the PSUs. They were only allowed to drive around looking hard and were not to be used to report crimes or get cats out of trees. Some came from small rural forces and had smart uniforms and funny accents. I gave it the full Cockney twat bit as you'd expect. Then during one shift I drove out of the station yard in my special Duty Officer police car and a Somalian woman and her two children waved at me and clapped. It was then that I realised what we did was really important and got a lump in my throat.

Early one summer's morning, at around 2.00-3.00am, a call went into the Central Command Complex (CCC) via the 999 system. Not all 999 calls are emergencies; the person who takes it is expected to decide on the relevant grading. True emergencies get immediate response. Lesser dramas, attendance within the hour.

That night a young man had just started his career with the Metropolitan Police. Working as a civilian member of staff, he was based at CCC in Hendon. It was his first night in call receipt and things were quiet with few if any calls to the police. But then once came in. From a landline at a residential address in a nice part of west London. An address covered by Acton Police.

He took the call and at first there was silence, until he heard a small voice, sounding far away, an elderly person perhaps, or a young child making no response to his questions. A mis-call? It happened a lot. Children accidentally dialled 999 sometimes, or a phone got knocked. These things happen. There was a routine at CCC to screen those sorts of calls out.

The young man kept trying, though. Nothing. Then a small voice again. He couldn't quite make out what they were saying. He wasn't sure. Was it a mistake? In the early hours of the morning someone dialled 999. There was something about it.

That young man, on his first day in the police service, made one of the most important decisions of his life. He decided to deploy police officers to the address as an emergency.

We were contacted at Acton Police Station: abandoned call traced to an address; comments the call handler thought he'd heard. Units to go on immediate response.

We had nothing else to do. All was quiet in old London Town so I went with three others, heading south, into the W4 postcode area normally known as Chiswick but covered by Ealing Council. It is smart and residential, expensive houses in walking distance of Chiswick High Street. A wealthy part of the Borough, it is little plagued with the sort of crime issues seen elsewhere, an enclave of ordinariness between Acton and Chiswick.

We found the address on a road in darkness, odd street light shining through aged trees lining the footpaths. Not a soul about.

The house had a small garden area, with a path leading up to a heavy wooden front door. We let the control room know we'd arrived. Attendance times were a key performance indicator, our then Chief Inspector Operations seemed to take pleasure in naming and shaming any Duty Officer whose team missed the Charter Times. And then the world changed.

We knocked on the door and almost simultaneously one PC noticed a smashed ground floor window. His torch showed it led into a front room that, like the rest of the house, was in darkness.

And then she screamed. A primeval sound, the base screech of a human being at the point of death, tearing into the stillness of the night. And then again. Same sound. We were kicking at the door, pounding, beating, our every instinct to get into that house because the screams were wrenching at our souls.

The door wouldn't go in. We kicked as hard as we could, but it remained locked solid. So we called for an enforcer, a big metal battering ram, and it was soon on its way with another police car, but they were miles away, might as well have been on the other side of the world. One of us tried to enter via the broken window, but the gap was too small, even trying to smash his way in with a baton couldn't change that. Until one upstairs window opened and somebody threw us some keys.

Soon we were heading into the darkness, on our way towards we knew not what, screaming still hammering our eardrums.

Two officers went upstairs and found her, an elderly lady in the front bedroom, the house racked with her sobs as the officers held her and told her she was safe. But she somehow found the energy to carry on screaming: 'He's still here ... he's got a knife...'

I went into the kitchen area, vaguely lit through the windows by a full moon in a cloudless sky, and there he was, face covered in his victim's underwear, long kitchen knife in hand. He dropped that as we took him to the ground and handcuffed him.

'I know my rights! I know my rights!' he yelled. 'I know my rights!' shouted the 55-year-old security guard, who had never been arrested in his life but had developed a crazed obsession.

She would shop by routine, passing through on a regular and predictable basis, allowing him to alter his shifts and change his ways so he would be able to follow her and find out where she lived. And when the night came, as the world slept and the only ones abroad were police and thieves, he broke into the home of a 77-year old woman and spent an hour inflicting the most evil acts on her body. She made that 999 call while he used her toilet.

'I know my rights!' he went on shouting in handcuffs. With her screams still ratcheting my soul, time stood still, I wanted to hurt him with all my being. But I didn't because that would make me the same as him, wouldn't it? That would make me him.

The ambulance crew arrived, helped her to dress and led her to the ambulance while we stood watching, smoking cigarettes, hands shaking. And she stopped to thank us. She said thank you.

I wished we'd got there earlier and caught him going in; that we'd been out on patrol in Chiswick instead of sitting around at Acton Police Station; and that we could have stopped this evil because that is what the police are supposed to do. We should have stopped this happening. A pit of despair opened within me.

The wheels of the criminal justice system duly turned and he was sent to prison for a mere twelve years.

He knew his rights.

Corruption Comes Home to Roost

I'd been a Duty Officer for five years. Working earlies, lates and nights. That's the insufferably early part of the day, then the bit when you should be in the pub, then the bit when you should be staggering home pished, sobbing your heart out because you recognised the futility of existence in the kebab shop queue.

Shift work doesn't do great things to you physically either. This is particularly notable as you stray into your older years. Emergency Response is the most mentally challenging area of police work, in a direct, immediate sense. And I'm proper thick, so it was time for a change again.

Being a Duty Officer did feel like proper police work, having a direct impact on real lives. Being a Detective Inspector again would be a step away from that, back into the dark undercurrent of number crunching and fighting internal battles. It turned out the role of Safer Neighbourhoods Inspector was due to become vacant at Southall. It held promise of more sociable hours and fewer people trying to gob in your mouth.

Safer Neighbourhoods had recently been re-named the Local Policing Teams. A penchant of police management is to give things a different name and pretend it's new and shiny when in fact it's just a shoddy paint job done by a mate of a mate. The Commissioner at the time had promised everyone that the Local Policing Teams would be at full strength. As there weren't enough cops to go around, several hundred were moved from response teams to staff up LPT. When it was time to promise all response teams would be at full strength, they were all moved back again. Double counting at its finest. Tea and commendations all round.

Ealing Borough was split in four – Acton, Greenford, Southall and Ealing. From high wealth to shameful poverty, each sector led by an Inspector. I got the Southall gig. The only applicant.

At first, I was keen to make a lasting impression in one of the biggest drugs markets in Britain. Gangs fought for control of a thriving sales pitch, cheap prices attracting users from across London. Thousands with immigration issues lived in beds in sheds, workers in an undeclared economy. Prostitution blighted Southall Broadway in the hours of darkness, a hideous contrast to a vibrant daytime street of sari shops and restaurants tempting crowds of shoppers.

Those women forced into selling their bodies came from backgrounds of abuse and drug addiction. The vast majority sustained heavy addictions to crack cocaine, abused by men who used them in alleyways ankle-deep in beer cans, syringes and discarded condoms. Some would be murdered because of their position in society, killed by the men who detested them.

After every death, a demand that something must be done bubbled up from management. I once tried to instigate a project in which kerb crawlers would be encouraged to desist via letters to their home address, but it never took off because all the care and compassion following the murder of a prostitute drains away pretty damn quickly. Truth is, nobody really cares about those women. There is no incentive, politically or within policing, to actually solve the problem. We could have made a difference, but all my officers were sent back to response duties to paper over the cracks opening up all over the Met.

The ship was sinking but the top brass all had their binoculars trained on the House of Lords.

A significant part of neighbourhood policing revolves around interaction with key members of the community. But the key question has always been 'who decides who the key members of the community are?' In policing circles it's usually the people who shout loudest or complain the most.

In Southall, the most influential types were connected to the various religious establishments, elected committee representatives mainly, who managed the enormous influence of their institution. Elections were bitterly fought and presented significant policing challenges. The participants were consummate politicians, well versed in seeking influence. Many had the personal contact number of officers senior to myself. A useful tool when I might not have taken a course of action they wished for.

Just before I arrived at Southall, someone called Paul Martin would take over as Borough Commander. He had come to Ealing Borough as a Superintendent and would be promoted in post to become a Chief Superintendent. He would later take charge of the three London Boroughs which would combine to form West Area. He was a corrupt police officer who would finally be sacked for gross misconduct in January 2022. He was held up by many sycophants and enablers and lasted far longer than he should.

Corrupt officers do not exist in isolation.

As the Southall Inspector, I would be contacted by local dignitaries who felt slighted by some matter or other. Should my response not meet their needs, I would quickly be called by a senior officer who had taken a call from the same person demanding I change my decision immediately. As a life-long sucker, I actually believed the old policing adage that 'integrity is non-negotiable'. This clearly didn't wash with others.

As always, such communications are never official. Nothing is ever recorded or sent in an email. It's cheeky little phone calls or quick chats in closed-door offices without coffee. Sometimes it was subtle. I was often told that Mr Martin wasn't happy about how things were going. I was never given specifics, even though I asked. I entertained myself by asking for support in my personal development, maybe by way of a development plan. Far be it from me not to keep a corrupt senior officer happy.

I felt a professional responsibility to the people of Southall. It is a most intriguing area and offered a unique challenge. I still felt I had a career in the Metropolitan Police Service at that point.

How deluded I was.

A key part of community engagement is engaging with the community and despite losing staff hand over fist, the demand on my officers at Southall continued to increase.

If there was a serious incident, we were the first to be called upon to do some community reassurance. This involved walking up and down in luminous jackets, making sure everyone knew that something serious had happened and that we'd be walking up and down to make sure it didn't happen again. Until we had to go walk up and down somewhere else, of course, then it would be another free-for-all.

Community officers were also directed to investigate lower level crimes on their patches. In Southall, there was a lot of crime. If a report had a 'named suspect' on it, the officer was expected to deal with this as a matter of priority. A lot of crimes had a lot of named suspects on them.

The Borough Detective Superintendent was in charge of

blaming junior officers for not progressing investigations with named suspects. If someone had not dealt with something as promptly as the Det Supt felt possible, he would accuse the officer of committing malfeasance in public office, a criminal offence. Taking no account of other pressures or demands, he would accuse a constable with less than a year's service of having done something that could potentially lead to a term of imprisonment.

The same delightful chap would chair the next meeting and demand to know why those same officers weren't walking up and down in bright jackets. At the same time as investigating crime and arresting suspects. I'd counter that he and his senior mates had taken all my staff to fill up response teams, and that it wasn't physically possible for the ones left behind to do everything. At which he called me a cheeky C-word.

Funny how the police service attracts those who gain sensual pleasure from demeaning and threatening people forced to call them sir. In another world, he'd have been the cowardly lion in an S&M parlour in Deptford. As I wish I'd told him at the time.

One day, a woman walked into Southall Police Station and set fire to the front office. Upon arrest, she was found in possession of a receipt from a local petrol station. This listed three items: Petrol can, petrol and matches. The receipt was signed off with the delightful rejoinder: HAVE A NICE DAY!

Well, I wasn't having a nice day. I had no staff and the Front Office was on fire.

The joy of working as a community Inspector was the freedom to develop projects and ideas. I met some fascinating people and learned about different places and cultures. It is a role I'd highly recommend but, as it has since been disbanded, you can't have a go I'm afraid.

Southall is famous for battering the National Front in 1978. Top job. It's also well known for religious festivals. The largest is the Sikh festival of Vaisakhi, where thousands of people parade through the cramped streets with great happiness. There's loads of free food and everyone is delighted to see you, a true break from regular policing. I enjoyed each and every one of these festivals and loved spending my days wandering around, talking to wonderful people and having photos taken with their families.

I also had the pleasure of meeting key community leaders, religious and secular. I was always warmly welcomed, although did feel uncomfortable on one occasion when a senior committee member expected me to take intrusive action against someone in Canada who'd been rude about him on Facebook. I explained that, generally, differences of opinion were a civil matter.

He leaned in said: 'Paul. The Sikh people will rise against you.'

'What, all of them?'

'Yes, Paul. All of them.'

'Okay. Thanks for letting me know.'

I made haste back to the police station and filled out a quick Community Impact Assessment. I thought it prudent to let the Met know that one of their Inspectors was the subject of an uprising by one of the world's great religions.

I once really annoyed our Borough Commander by going on a three-month attachment to the Prince's Trust charity as a DI at Acton. It was just before I flounced off to uniform, so it seemed like a nice thing to do. Having spent most of the year on courses to get promoted and leave the Borough himself, he accused me of disloyalty and failing the people of Ealing, irony not his strong point. A small chap, he needed a stepladder to browbeat people, so I dealt with his criticisms by being six foot three inches tall.

I spent three months working with young people in South London who were then defined as NEETS: not in employment, education or training. It was the longest time I'd spent away from police officers since flogging records and it was eye-watering. I caught myself in my flies on my first day.

The work confirmed my belief that young people are not the

enemy. They are going to have to inherit the world we've fucked up, so let's all be a bit nicer to them. One might be a divine being on his second visit, so it's best to cover all bases.

I wanted to work in Southall schools, and my chance came when I was approached by a headmaster worried about students being radicalised. I had no idea what to do, a recurring theme. I phoned up someone in the Counter Terrorism Command who wouldn't tell me his name. I expected that, it just amused me to ask. He told me to fucking do one, so I phoned someone much nicer and they gave me info on a new project being trialled.

I ended up getting this fella who was massive on YouTube to come to a high school in Southall to do a presentation where he'd take the piss out of terrorists. I stood at the back of the hall as it filled with young people. They had no idea what was going on, so I felt an affinity with them. Then the main man came on stage, and the place went mental. I got swept up in the excitement and started screaming. He really was a big star and his message was amazing. I am confident he worked wonders that day and had a lasting impression on everyone who saw him.

I have his autograph, which is currently on sale on eBay. It's on my favourite police trousers too, so is a premium-priced item.

I got in contact with another school and offered to cure them of radicalisation by having a bloke off YouTube do crude jokes them write his name on their trousers. I remember the gentle click as the receiver was carefully replaced.

Then there was the high school careers day at which I was expected to discuss police service careers. I asked if any student had expressed interest in corruption, which led to an awkward silence, and ended up doing a presentation about the time we charged the wrong bloke with murder, which they really liked in a pretty psychotic way, demanding the suspect be hung. They were surprised the death penalty had been repealed and swore to lobby for its return. As I revealed that the man charged turned out to be the wrong man, they dug their heels in and stated that their decision remained correct. Sensing that I'd done more harm than good, I shared some cigarettes around and went home.

Corruption gets everywhere. It's not tackled because there's no political will or support to do so. You don't get lateral career development or promotional opportunities by standing up to it. It has the opposite effect, making officers far more willing to turn a blind eye or move. The size of the Met makes this more likely.

One day at Southall, I popped to Greggs to get lunch, as one does. Making the worst decision of my career, I decided to return to my desk rather than eat in. That wasn't through dedication. All the seats were taken by drug users.

My office was on the first floor of the station, overlooking the teeming high street. My walls were adorned with indie music posters and my screen saver was Sonic Youth's *Goo* album cover to show what an alternative, edgy Police Inspector I really was.

Next door was the Detective Sergeant's office. My usual DS was off sick, had been for some time, unable to return any time soon. Another officer there had worked in the CID once upon a time and kindly agreed to fill the role on an Acting Detective Sergeant basis to try and stop the whole place sinking.

One of my other Sergeants, meanwhile, was a close friend of Paul Martin, the Chief Superintendent mentioned earlier, fired for bullying staff and filing bogus expenses claims as ruled by the Met's Directorate of Professional Standards in 2022. The pair went to family events together, worked closely, and he was often unavailable for work at Southall. This bloke spread discord and, I was convinced, was briefing both against me and his supposed colleagues at Southall. It seemed we were all on the metaphorical non-corrupt naughty chair for not playing Martin's game.

Also in January 2022, this mate of Martin's was found to have breached 'Standards of Professional Behaviour amounting to misconduct, in relation to, orders and instructions, duties and responsibilities, and authority, respect and courtesy.' Although allowed to keep his job, he was 'issued with management advice'.

A third man, Chief Inspector Davinder Kandohla, was like Paul Martin dismissed without notice.

Anyway, the rise of my Southall officer to the role of Acting Detective Sergeant didn't go down well with those three. In fact it caused anger. I was ordered to make sure he wore a uniform, even though the majority of his work was office-based. This became a real issue and I sensed something fishy. I hoped it was a flash in the pan; little did I know it would lead to my downfall.

Missing People and a World Weary Detective

I'd been collecting evidence of my work in the local community with a view to applying for promotion to Chief Inspector. Work on neighbourhoods was well known for producing evidence to support promotion, and I felt it was the right time in my career.

I sent three pages of A4 evidence on a Personal Development Record (PDR) form to my line manager for endorsement or otherwise, but didn't hear anything further. I later found that my PDR had been altered. All the evidence was deleted and replaced by two paragraphs holding me responsible for an incident between Martin's mate and our Acting Detective Sergeant saying I should have dealt with it better. I should not have involved my line manager but as an experienced Inspector dealt with it myself. My poor management should exclude me from promotion.

This PDR version was submitted without my knowledge and indeed scuppered any future career I felt I might have.

At the time, I was on a flexible working pattern to support my family life. I had a wife who worked and children who didn't. The Met took pride in supporting flexible working and numerous official policies lauded this aim. The day before the Notting Hill Carnival, at which I was set to work, my line manager told me my days at Southall were over. I'd go back to being a Duty Officer on full hours doing shifts. This was in breach of the flexible working policy, but came as no surprise. It wasn't the relentless targeting by a corrupt regime that finally got me, it was the idea that I wasn't going to be able to look after my children.

Previously, I'd been refused paternity leave following the birth of my daughter because my then line manager didn't want to pay overtime to get a Sergeant to carry out my role over the weekend. Getting kicked off flexible working wasn't really a surprise, but it just added to everything else and overwhelmed me.

I had a mental breakdown. The doctors put me on the sort of pills mad people get put on and documented that I was suffering from stress and depression caused by work. I was off sick for some months. I had finally been defeated.

Being off sick from the police with a mental health condition is a rum old business. I'd never been treated for my age-old PTSD, and still had dreams about people dying in burning buildings. Being engulfed in corruption didn't help.

I'd previously done a bit of writing and felt it helped. For example, I'd written an opinion piece in *The Guardian* once, using an assumed name to cleverly throw the stalkers in blue serge off my scent. My views on senior officers seemed worthy of print in everyone's favourite slightly-left of centre broadsheet.

I'd written a blog around the same time, the World Weary Detective, and ended up getting online threats from the far right.

One, who called himself White Wolf's Cock or something, spent the night spewing filth at me and then signed off with a profuse apology. I imagined he'd been caught by his mother coming into the basement to ask about the stains down the back of her dress.

I stopped blogging, however, when someone at Scotland Yard wrote something really unpleasant on the Met intranet about officers not being allowed to be human on the internet via the medium of blog. I assumed that meant me. I saw it as a vital point of principle to stand by my own beliefs, so immediately gave up. I didn't cry though, which I think is an important point to make.

Policing offers refuge for the Alpha male, many of whom seek high office to make up for the missing parts of their personality. It has long been accepted that it has an impact on mental health. It is little accepted that this may actually mean people need help. Mental health issues in the police are seen as a sign of weakness.

I turned vegetarian and joined the Labour Party. Most police officers prefer three word slogans which usually involve the word 'leftie' as a base insult. I found local Labour activists to be a most humourless bunch who kept going on about some God figure called Jeremy. I assumed they'd all gone to public school together, so left before I spontaneously combusted.

I'd been a vegetarian before, just before my blood sugar level dropped so low I fell over in a petrol station and fractured my skull. I found my redemption in KFC. All praise the Colonel!

I also qualified in Druidry which helped a bit, but still needed an outlet so turned to comedy and surreal diatribes. Time was spent sitting in Woking library wearing headphones and giggling to myself. I fitted right in. Then I read some autobiographies by famous comedians to give me something to dribble over.

My Name is Daphne Fairfax: A Memoir, by Arthur Smith, found its way to me. It turned out Arthur's dad, Syd Smith, was a copper in London after the war. He worked in Kennington as well. Something told me that we had something in common. I wasn't hearing voices – it was an audiobook.

I went on social media and Tweeted at Arthur. Like a twat. He responded. I imagine he still regrets that decision to this day. I sent him my writing and he asked to meet me and have lunch. I asked a responsible adult to confirm this was indeed his intention and not a figment of my imagination. Being off sick with mental health issues wouldn't exempt me from prosecution for stalking a Comedy Store original.

I ended up reading my scribblings to a select audience in Arthur's south London flat. Then I drank wine and chatted like a grown-up who wasn't a mental copper on the sick. It was suggested I consider stand-up, so I blagged a gig at an arts centre. Arthur agreed to appear for free. I suspect this may have been why I got the gig, but I don't want to spoil things for myself.

I made my stand-up debut in front of 120 people. Which was a real turn-up. Nobody was violently sick or tried to hit me, so I judged it a success. I got all high and mighty after that and wrote a stage show. I cleverly named it, *You're Nicked You Slag* and performed it at fringe festivals across the country while dressed as Margaret Thatcher. Some people gave me money and it wasn't to pop to the shops for sweets.

I made sure it was all registered as a business interest with the police, so I wasn't doing any corruption, even though corruption was the flavour of the season in Ealing Borough at the time.

Then I had to go back to work.

On my return, I was served paperwork saying if I went sick again, Unsatisfactory Performance Procedures would be instigated, which could lead to my dismissal. I argued that I was off sick with a mental illness caused directly by my treatment at work, and produced medical documents to support this. These were ignored, no surprise to anyone, and I was told to sign the forms.

My sick record meant I was unable to apply for other roles away from Ealing Borough or to apply for promotion. Even if my

PDR hadn't been altered, my career was over, defeated by a corrupt cabal for daring to stand against them. I waved my hands in the air; I waved them like I just didn't care!

I was still on medication.

Back on shift work at Ealing Police Station, though, in charge of another response team and making critical decisions, this time on mad pills. I suspected I was being set up to fail but, admittedly, that might have been the hallucinations.

As a Duty Officer, one of my responsibilities was dealing with people who called in to complain. The Senior Leadership Team was assessed on the number of formal complaints their Borough recorded. The unwritten (obviously) idea was that Inspectors could talk people out of making formal complaints and help the seniors get their next rank while taking the blame if things went wrong. Well, I wasn't playing that game. I made sure every complaint was formally recorded and submitted. I was informally told to stop it but must have had some sort of short-term memory issue based on my medication, so didn't.

Then a man called in to complain about being arrested. He'd beaten up his wife, which he admitted, and was given a police caution after having had legal advice from a solicitor. He didn't like being arrested. I had a sense of humour failure, as you'd imagine. We're all human after all. The wife-beater and I didn't hit it off, to be honest. He told me he was going to come down to the police station and set himself on fire. I hung up. As one does. He then phoned up to complain about me, and I was summonsed to see a Chief Inspector.

Although well versed in the ways of the Ealing SLT, I was still surprised when given formal words of advice for being rude to a wife beater – by hanging up the phone. My disciplinary record, colourful as it was, was extended by a finding of guilt for being rude to a wife beater. At least it was over the phone so my haughty manner while seated couldn't have caused further upset.

I argued that I was suffering from mental health problems

caused by work, but was told to piss off and get on with it. I swallowed my pride and medication and left the building. Then came back five minutes later. I remembered I was still on duty.

It wasn't the last pop they'd have at me. Not by a long shot.

One of many bows to a Duty Inspector's stringed instrument is dealing with missing people, a thorny and risky business indeed. People go AWOL for all sorts of reasons, many not known to the officers called to deal with it. The Duty Officer decides whether the risk to the missing person is low, medium or high.

If the risk is low, the police do bugger all. If medium, the police pretend to do something but as so many persons disappear at the same time, along with other demands, this usually also equates to bugger all. If the risk is high, the Duty Officer has an almighty row with the duty Detective Sergeant who thinks *The Sweeney* was a documentary and doesn't understand the concept of rank. Then the CID step in because they're told to. Wankers.

One Friday I took over from the late turn Duty Officer, who was hiding in a filing cabinet. It was silly busy and, due to it being 10.00pm, most of the Met were snuggled in with their teddy. An officer came for a risk assessment, one adult female gone missing. She'd done similar before, leaving a friend in charge of her kids. She was also a competitive kick boxer. Medium risk, I thought.

After two days off, I came in to an email shared between some of us Duty Officers from the Detective Superintendent. 'That misper [missing person] from the weekend. It's a murder.' I'd no idea what he was talking about, because we have a lot of missing people (and I was mental). It turned out the poor woman had been killed by a male acquaintance, dead by the time she'd been reported missing.

As policing Ealing Borough isn't *Minority Report* I had no idea she was at risk of being killed when doing my initial risk assessment, but this didn't wash with dear old Ealing SLT. I was referred to the Independent Office for Police Conduct, my actions potentially having contributed to her death. The IOPC investigates coppers for serious wrongs and I was formally notified I was under investigation five months after the incident. Yes, five months later. I was called to see a Superintendent and formally notified of the investigation. Hilariously, I then had ten days to respond and if I failed to do that it would be held against me. I did indeed chuckle loudly at the irony. The Superintendent looked relieved to escape the room without having to use restraint techniques.

I was summonsed for interview under caution, having sought advice from my Police Federation representative who was also, handily, a Sergeant on my response team. He asked the IOPC if I was being treated as a suspect and, if not, why was I being interviewed under criminal caution?

As a seasoned detective, I knew that there was, literally, no evidence that I was a criminal suspect in anything and the IOPC kindly agreed. They were fishing, as it's called. Not that they'd admit it. If they hadn't agreed, I'd have stuck a couple of pencils up my nose and sat on the roof in my underpants. There were a couple of coppers up there already, so I'd have made friends.

I was sent a questionnaire instead, asking why I'd not treated her as a high risk missing person, among other things. As is always the case, no reference was made to other demands on me at the time, or why my predecessor was hiding in a filing cabinet. There was also no reference to the SLT failures to provide me with sufficient staff to meet minimum staffing levels, or provide sufficient support to properly investigate missing persons cases as demanded by official Met policies and procedures.

I wasn't able to blame strategic failures, or the SLT. It was for the SLT to blame me. You'd think I'd have worked that one out by now, wouldn't you?

I told the IOPC that I didn't grade her as high risk because I didn't know she was dead. My Fed Rep advised that I remove some swear words from my response, and I submitted it. So three months later and after eight months of investigation the IOPC decided I had no case to answer.

I'm sure Ealing SLT could have worked it out for themselves. Wonder why they didn't?

Surreal Times in the Metropolitan Police

D Team were amazing. Not just due to my leadership, but it was a key part, as no-one ever told me. They were a team of caring, brave individuals, who were sadly working for a corrupt Borough Commander and a Duty Inspector who was mental. And not in a funny, wacky way either. But I tried. Dear God, I tried.

Here is a story of heroism to cheer ourselves up. It's important to remember the police are here for the nasty things in life.

One early shift we were relaxing when a call came in. An old domestic violence panic alarm had been set off in a block of flats. Everyone groaned, but a few coppers volunteered. I was looking at them under my eyebrows, so I can claim some credit for that.

The woman who pressed the alarm did so for a reason. She'd

managed to escape for a few seconds from her estranged partner who'd broken in. He'd been there for some hours, drinking and taking drugs, and had armed himself with a kitchen knife.

My officers arrived and all hell broke loose, a statement I am aware I've written a few times. By now, Body Worn Video had become general issue to front-line officers, a wonderful piece of kit providing impactive evidence and reminding us actually to use a caution rather than just say you did in post-arrest statements.

They managed to force entry into the flat by smashing the door down. The suspect grabbed the toddler and retreated to the kitchen. He ended up with his knife to the throat of his own child, threatening to slice it in front of the approaching officers. The incident was captured on video and I can honestly say it is the most amazing piece of footage I've ever seen.

The officers enter the kitchen, the man silhouetted against the window, bright morning sunshine lighting dust particles around his head. He holds the child, hooked in his left hand, the boy's head lolled across his chest, the knife pressed to his throat. There is a pause, a matter of seconds, as the officers realise he intends to slice the throat of his own kid. He is shaking, moving the knife from side to side, while screaming threats.

Then, as one, the officers charge at him. In seconds, they are upon him. One grasps the wrist holding the knife and bends it away from the youngster's throat just long enough for another officer to grab the child and pull him downwards. He then turns and throws the child across the room to another officer who catches him in her arms, before turning and assisting his colleague in forcibly disarming the knifeman, who is making every effort to stab them.

The child was given to his sobbing mother on the balcony outside as other officers arrived.

Later investigation by the CID into the man's background, combined with the woman's statement, revealed he'd gone there that morning with the express intention of killing them both.

While officers were performing astounding acts of bravery, the cabal of corruption continued unabated. Around this time, the BCU model had been brought in. Due to the fact that policing was sinking and response teams were regularly under strength, someone got a promotion by deciding to merge Boroughs, so we could all sink together.

Ealing merged with Hillingdon to the west and Hounslow to the south to form West Area. Ealing was the best because it had more calls to police than the other two put together. I'm not one for stats, because I'm numerically illiterate, but do like a bit of one-upmanship. Hillingdon had the dubious pleasure of being more unsuccessful than Ealing in performance indicators. And it was a proper weird place. Not as weird as Hounslow, though. Hounslow covers posh Chiswick, home of many famous people, and Feltham, the area with the UK's highest rate of inbreeding.

Hillingdon and Hounslow had two extremely decent men as Borough Commanders, so the powers that be decided to make Ealing's Paul Martin BCU Commander.

There were focus groups and I, along with everyone else who actually did police work, argued the BCU proposal was utterly ridiculous. We were, as expected, totally ignored, and the policy wonks won the day. The Senior Leadership Team got to give themselves shiny new titles.

There was to be a command structure. One of the three Duty Inspectors would fill the role of Silver Commander West Area from a Control Room within Hounslow Police Station. A Local Operating Procedure was written. I can't recall the exact wording, but basically stating that Silver was to take the blame for every decision, all reviewed by a member of the SLT after the incident concluded. Handy, eh? The SLT actually designated themselves 'platinum' in the policy. I ask you. Platinum? Someone had been watching too much *Star Trek*. Nice for the Inspectors to have responsibility for a population the size of Birmingham though.

Anyway, despite all objections the BCU became the Holy Grail. Taxpayers' money was used to create banners showing fake coppers enjoying life on the BCU with perfect white teeth. A lot of lies were told about minimum staffing and how our response teams were up to strength, while we sat in a room with a handful of nervous coppers and one of those cardboard cut-outs they use in the window of Poundland to scare away shoplifters.

If us Duty Officers, when not being Sooper Dooper Silver Commanders, had the audacity to complain, we were told it isn't actually about the numbers of officers you have on any one day, it's what we do with them. A bit like penises.

I was ordered to change my way of thinking from considering too few police officers a risk to the general public. In moments of reflection, I understood why I wasn't up to being a member of the SLT. Then I flushed, washed my hands, and got on with it.

We were entering our final few months as an independent policing nation.

These were surreal times in the Metropolitan Police and not just because I was heavily medicated. Here are some other stories, written in a public library while wearing headphones.

And I'm not even dribbling.

Dealing with a double stabbing at an illegal rave in Ealing, I found myself entering into a discussion with some young chaps about the drumming abilities of Phil Collins and the bass playing of Mark King of Level 42. They were astounded to hear that I had lived through those times and we left on the best of terms.

At another rave, I felt it necessary to call in the dear old Territorial Support Group. I'd had an officer assess the numbers to allow me to conduct a risk assessment. He was barely literate, but beggars can't be choosers. He assessed there were too many people ravin' for us to deal with locally. My normal stance was the use of verbal commands such as, 'fuck off home, it's a school night.' My admonishments fell on deaf ears, so I knew we had a fight on our hands. Either that or the music was too loud and they couldn't hear me.

We were allowed to use the Commissioners Reserve after I promised them the chance to have a scrap. I set an RVP, which they drove past. As they always did. Every. Fucking. Time. After a massive screeching U-turn, they all got out in their riot dressing up gear and stood in a big group flexing and pouting.

I had to contact the Duty Superintendent for authority for something or other. He was a really big man who turned up in a really small car with another Superintendent. I made a joke about buses. The second boss was part of a new scheme whereby people who'd never done any policing at all decided that other people who'd never done any policing at all could join the police at Inspector or Superintendent ranks and tell us mere mortals what the bloody hell to do. The Direct Entry Superintendent was an ex-teacher so I got her to mark my homework before the briefing. Looking at the TSG she said, 'and what do these chaps do?'

'They kick people's heads in ma'am,' I said, before walking away in a patronising manner.

One of the many duties of a Met response team is to provide a car with two coppers in it to drive around looking at important addresses. Such addresses are usually the homes of people who've upset people in big sunglasses who live abroad, or else places that terrorist types might fancy blowing up. The same vehicle is also responsible for dealing with suspect packages and thereby called the Bomb Car. If somone calls the police and expresses concern about an abondoned suitcase at a bus stop for example, the Bomb Car will be sent super fast. The coppers will then decide if the object is a bomb by kicking it. If they can't make the assessment without losing a limb, they'll pester the Duty Inspector who'll send the Bomb Squad with its robots and annoying mannerisms.

Ealing. One evening, someone answered their door in one of the big houses. A shifty character asked if he could plug a device into their outside plug socket. I had no idea that posh houses had plugs on the front. You learn something new every day.

The householders cast stereotypical judgement on the shady wrong 'un at their door and sent them away with a Cruft's flea in their ear. So they went to the next house and plugged something in. The original householder ordered their butler to call the police, so our Bomb Car turned out.

Most embassies are in central London. There is no British Embassy in London. I had an officer who worked for me call directory enquiries and ask, so can confirm this. North Korea, ever the contrarians, have theirs in Ealing – a house on the North Circular Road that used to be owned by Sid James. I should imagine that's what sold it to them. Cor blimey, nya, nya, nya!

It was the dwelling on the other side of this embassy that suddenly had a suspect device attached to it. Which was a worry. I heard the location and immediately cracked open my copy of 'A Dummies Guide to Explosive Shit' which showed that if said device went off, it would cause consternation in Pyongyang.

The occupants of the embassy did not engage with the police, so were designated 'anti', as in anti-police, a designation that basically covered everyone who had ever had the misfortune of having dealings with the Met.

They'd got angry with a local barber who'd offered customers the same funny haircut as sported by their Dear Leader too, so I suspected they were on edge. Having their Embassy blown up might start World War Three. I imagined the SLT would try to pin that on me in my Personal Development Review as well.

So our designated Bomb Car turned up to have a gander at the suspect device and decided it didn't look right at all, before knocking at the address to get the occupants out. It was then that they got attacked by a German Shepherd.

More police types arrived and frankly made things worse. The dog was secured and the owners told to fuck off. Or something like that. A van was seen nearby, so a couple of officers went to make enquiries and ended up in a fight with a gang of burglars living in the back. A third police car turned up and realised that something was amiss. One colleague was in the back of an ambulance, another two were having a dust-up in the back of a Transit, and the official car of the Ambassador of North Korea couldn't get into their Embassy because the Metropolitan Police Service had parked across the gates.

I don't know why, but they called me to the scene. I was the only supervisor on duty, apart from one Acting Sergeant I hadn't spoken to in months after he managed to smash the passenger window of the Duty Officer's car with a colleague's head.

On arrival, I ordered the North Circular closed. Just because I could really. I was then approached by a really polite chap who said he worked for the ambassador and asked that we kindly move the police car from North Korean soil. I said his English was really great in a loud voice. He repeated his question and I felt we were at risk of nuclear catastrophe, so had the car moved while the Koreans went inside and slammed the door.

Then I remembered the supposed explosive device. I found a probationer and told them to knock on the door and ask them to evacuate. Embassies being officially the land of the country concerned, we had no official powers. I'd have done it myself but was worried I might get trapped inside as some kind of political prisoner. I told the probbie that if there were any problems he should leg it across the back gardens.

Luckily the North Korean diplomats kindly agreed to stand on the opposite side of the road, but only within sight of their front door. The burglars from the van were looking shifty.

Someone at Scotland Yard got wind of what I was up to and wished to hear more. They took over the radio channel and started using weird code words. They asked what my command structure was. I said, 'Me and an Acting Sergeant, but we ain't talking.' They asked that the role of Bronze Cordons be allocated and an RVP formed for central units with a forward briefing station. I broke my silence and asked my colleague to go and hang around Ealing Common and wave at police cars when they turned up. I told him he was Bronze Cordons, but he wasn't getting a sash. Not on my watch.

Scotland Yard sent the TSG, so I told them to keep the fuck away from everything. If there's one police unit that's likely to start a war, it's the bloody TSG. They missed the RVP anyway, and I didn't tell them to stop. They're probably still driving west.

The Bomb Squad turned up and parked in a very macho way. The first officer on the scene was called over and asked to do a sketch. This is so they can form a view of what sort of device they are dealing with before deciding on a plan of action. The officer drew a picture of the house ... roof, four windows, a door and everything ... it was ace. Floella Benjamin would have loved it. The Bomb Squad didn't. He'd missed out the actual device.

How cross were the Bomb Squad! They thought he was taking the piss. Then they blew the device up. I assume this was protocol and not because they were showing us what they'd do if we annoyed them again with silly drawings. I'd imagine the watching North Koreans learned some new naughty words that day.

The North Korean Ambassador shook my hand and thanked me for my actions, thereby placing me on an MI5 watchlist.

As things settled down, I took a call. It was some Scotland Yard head honcho effusive in his praise. A lot of serious people had been monitoring what was going on. *A lot*, he emphasised. I did suggest they'd have been more than welcome to come down and take over, but he thought I was joking. He said I deserved a Commendation. I asked if he'd write it as Ealing SLT wouldn't and he carefully replaced the receiver. We never spoke again.

I was right in one thing. The SLT were about as likely to recommend me for a Commendation as rocking horse shite might fly over the moon. So I wrote my own. The PCs who attended and caused such chaos deserved mention. I didn't include the Bomb Squad because they were so rude.

Months later, I went to a BCU Commendation ceremony in some weird building in Ealing. Paul Martin stood up and talked about himself for so long I considered feigning a stroke. Then the bloke who owned the building talked about himself. Then a woman from an organisation nobody had heard of talked about herself before giving the soon-to-be disgraced Martin an award.

I'd forgotten how important Commendation ceremonies were to give credit and thanks to all the junior officers who'd risked their lives to do amazing things.

After that tedious shite, the actual ceremony began. Martin gave out commendations to his special friends and they all got bottles of champagne for their wives too. Finally, it was my turn. I was being a rebel, not wearing a tie. It's the little things that really stick it to the man. I had a photo taken with him, for which he put his arm around my waist and said he hoped it wasn't too tight. I said I found it quite a turn on, actually. If looks could kill!

Alas, I don't have a copy of the photo. We were told we had to pay for our own.

Lies, Damn Lies, and Senior Police Officers

While my wonderful response team were out doing amazingly brave and demonstrably stupid things, the cabal of corruption was forging onwards.

Paul Martin had decided to keep his operations at Ealing now that he was in charge of a vast swath of west London. It really was jobs for the boys! Our former Southall colleague was suddenly a Staff Officer as were a lot of other people. Enough to fill an entire floor of a police station. The nepotism was hiding in plain sight.

Officers were hand-picked to make sure his fantasy island was fully staffed. There were women involved. I imagine the promise of good evidence for promotion and lateral progression drew some decent people into his web of wrongness. It turned out he spent his time bullying and berating people who didn't treat him in the manner to which he'd become accustomed. Like the big man he really was. If you came up against this, you were kicked off the BCU. I had asked to be moved when I was threatened with being sacked for being mental, but it hadn't worked. Perhaps their work with me wasn't done.

Some officers bought enthusiastically into the whole thing. Helping hands were offered in the promotion stakes, temporary roles in a higher rank for those who couldn't be bothered to follow the official route. A lovely little pay rise and still chance for overtime in their official rank! Wowzers!

The front car park at Ealing Police Station was designated for their exclusive use. Actual police cars had to be left in side streets. Real police officers doing shift work had to park miles away.

One morning, we came in to find our night duty response friends had decided to reclaim the car park for the indigenous vehicles. Then one of Martin's friends, a Temporary Inspector and therefore properly important, came to work and parked his own car across the entrance before calling you know who to say what the nasty real police had gone and done. An emergency call came in and we had to ask him, most kindly, to move his vehicle so we could go and police it with police cars.

Paul Martin called the night duty Inspector at home and was nasty and rude. The cabal never had their car park nicked again.

This was all very amusing, but it did stick in the craw when I was trying to run a response team on 50 per cent strength.

Luckily for the world, before getting the old heave-ho, Martin managed to travel to Florida to take part in a conference. Quite what they thought he'd offer I have no idea. As the *Daily Mail* later reported it, he was alleged to have spent around £5,500 on a junior colleague's corporate credit card (you can likely guess which one), treating himself to upgraded flights, alcohol and treats from a 7/11 store before signing off the 'expenses' for said Sergeant when he got back to Ealing. Ker-fucking-ching!

I know. What was a Sergeant doing with a corporate credit card? Don't worry, he was a Temporary Inspector by that point, so there's nothing to see. Move along, please. Said a lot of people in the Met, who should have actually done something about it.

I reported every single thing the cabal did. Every. Single. Thing. If the Directorate of Professional Standards did loyalty points I'd have a caravan in Great Yarmouth by now. Other officers were doing the same. False allegations were made to the DPS against a senior officer as a result. They tried to fit him up for standing up to them. A classic tactic of the morbidly corrupt.

I got told I was an agitator. Which I quite liked. Better than being called a four-eyed ginger over the garden wall.

Being sent on aid to central London often felt like a respite break from the corruption of Ealing. I was most excited to be told I was going to protect Donald Trump. I really hoped to bump into Floella Benjamin and show her my officer's picture of the house next to North Korea's Embassy. Then I could shout 'THROUGH THE SQUARE WINDOW!' before high-fiving my PCs.

I saw Joanna Lumley in Soho once, while I was sitting in a police carrier. She waved at me and I came over all funny. The youngsters didn't have a clue who she was, so I made them walk around and around Trafalgar Square until they were sick

Trump had been threatening North Korea on Twitter, so I felt I truly had a role to play. I'd averted war with the Koreans once and could do it again. I brought it up at the briefing, but the Secret Service agent just did this funny thing with his face.

We were to wear our police helmets and yellow jackets and drive around Regent's Park in a converted transit as part of the overall security operation. I suspect we weren't that high in the food chain. Trump was staying in the American Ambassador's pad in the park, hence why we were there. I did think it might be a wind-up. I still smart from the time I thought I was meeting my Hendon classmates for a reunion but found the address to be a leather dungeon in Soho. I waited ages and not one of the gimps got a round in. To be fair, it *is* a bit tricky when you're suspended from the ceiling by your nipples.

The muster area was right next to a wall. The supervisors were told, in no uncertain terms, that if anyone, including police officers, went over that wall they'd be shot dead by American Special Forces. The PCs on my bus had really annoyed me on the trip across from Ealing, whinging on and constantly asking if we were there yet, so I thought about not telling them. I imagined lobbing their mobiles over the wall then ducking for cover.

We were aware that a really hilarious idea had sprung up on social media. People were encouraged to come to the area and bang pots and pans to keep Trump awake. Oh, my sides. In the end, only about ten turned out. And some orthodox Jews who stood and stared at the middle-class lads banging their Le Creuset. Strange old business.

Then, in the early hours, the radio suddenly burst into life. I unpeeled my face from the window and listened in. Some unit that sounded really covert was informing control that a car was acting suspiciously near a gate into Trump's home from home. Three men were trying to look over the wall.

It sounded very suspicious. It was suggested they might be terrorist assassins, or guerrilla gardeners or something. I was only barely awake. There was more firepower in Regent's Park that night that most of western Europe combined, so they chose us to tackle the terrorists. I piped up quickly, to check for understanding. We were humble bobbies with metal sticks and winning smiles. The powers-that-be brooked no argument. If the suspects produced big fuck off guns, then, and only then, would consideration be given to considering thinking about an armed deployment. It was the British way.

Then events took a surprising twist. The suspect car was coming towards us and the driver was really scowling. So we rammed it. Then we all got out and started shouting. Once the three men inside had gotten over their fright and had a nice cup of tea, I took their details and phoned secret people. I asked if these men had committed any offences under the Terrorism Act, a notoriously complicated piece of serious legislation that I'd had had little dealings with. My day job involved people threatening to batter neighbours for putting their bins out on the wrong day.

The secret person said they didn't have a clue, but apologised really nicely. They didn't say sorry for potentially having us killed, but that's water under the bridge in the finest traditions of the Metropolitan Police.

We were a bit flummoxed, so let them go. We pottered back and met real-life Secret Service Agents who wore shades in the dark and everything. They decided that the three men in the car would be banned from ever entering the United States. They asked what the UK response would be. I told them that I'd used a really stern voice with them. They seemed lost for words.

At the end of the shift, we were waiting to be dismissed. I'm not at my best at such times to be honest, especially if I haven't been to the toilet for ages. I'm thankful to the local resident who took the time to complain about the road closures and decided to tell me how exactly the security of the President of the United States should be dealt with.

I love meeting local experts. I felt like telling her so, but took a selfie instead. That really threw her, so she walked away with a strange look on her face. Job done. As they say.

Downfall of an Online Satirist

Having been forced back to work and threatened with the sack for going sick, I kept writing things I thought were funny to keep my head balanced. Using my own name, I put stuff online. A few magazines published my short stories. Then I wrote some gentle satire: 'A Guide to the British Police.' Little did I know it would lead to my final downfall in the Metropolitan Police. Here it is, with apologies for any jokes you may have already read in these pages. They are my own, so I can't be done for copyright:

> *Today's policing is nasty and brutish. And short, ever since a height requirement was abolished to provide employment outside panto season.*
>
> *This is a guide to policing in the real world; everything you need to know about the boys and girls in blue.*

I've been a police person for loads of years, so know what I'm talking about. I'm also a proper senior officer, so I'm never wrong.

The police contain two sorts of people — men and women. I have worked with both during my career. Police officers can be readily identified by other police officers. The trick is to look for the ones balancing a silly pointy hat on their head. Others will have a variety of pips and crowns or stripes on their shoulders designating rank. The higher the rank, the higher the level of self-regard. You are promoted by people with even higher levels of self-regard than your own.

In London, the rank structure is slightly different to elsewhere. We have Commanders. Nobody knows what Commanders do, but they all live together at headquarters. Above Commanders are Deputy Assistant Commissioners, Assistant Commissioners and head honcho, the Commissioner. All these people want to be the Commissioner, so they spy on each other and tell the Commissioner tales to get one up on each other. Commanders and above get their own cars with a driver. When they get promoted, they are given a shiny catalogue and model cars to push around to help them choose. The cars are fitted with blue lights hidden in the front grills and two-tone horns in case anyone ever needs a Commander on the hurry up.

Nobody ever needs a Commander on the hurry up.

Each London Borough has a Chief Superintendent in charge. They are known as Borough Commanders but are not Commanders. They just like the name because it is the best one. They are in charge of the Senior Leadership Team, which consists of Superintendents and Chief Inspectors. The Chief Inspectors all want to be Superintendents so make the tea all the time and are the designated drivers at Christmas and birthdays.

The Senior Leadership Team used to be called the Senior

Management Team (SMT) but they were often mistaken for the Safer Neighbourhood Team (SNT) so this was changed. Senior officers are far too important to deal with dog poo. The SLT meets every two weeks in a secret location where they wear flowing robes and blame Inspectors for everything.

Police officers also wear different coloured helmets in public order situations. If you want to lob a brick at an Inspector, aim for the red helmet. He'll be well behind the lines, so have a good throwing arm. You'll need some kind of projectile launcher if you wish to hit a more senior rank. They will be surrounded by runners and advisers though, so if hitting a sycophant is good enough, you'll have quite a wide target area. Be careful not to hit the fire brigade by mistake. It might wake them up.

Some police officers don't wear uniform. Some are engaged in deep level covert undercover work, so even a small piece of uniform can lead to disaster. Shoulder epaulettes on white shirts are a dead giveaway in gang circles. Standard plain clothes work is somewhat different. Here, an officer will don a North Face jacket, blue Levi jeans and Timberland boots. White-faced and with cropped hair, they will then stand outside Brixton tube station wondering why nobody is offering them drugs.

Police conduct surveillance in plain clothes. It would be silly not to. Lower level more amateur levels of surveillance are easily compromised. A colleague spent ten hours in the back of a van watching a drug dealer's address. Exiting the van after seeing no activity of any sort, he was surprised to see 'POLICE SURVEILLANCE VAN' spray-painted across the side. The van stayed in use for two more years as no-one could agree where a re-spray budget should come from.

On another occasion, a suspected car thief was arrested and taken into an unmarked police van by officers in plain clothes. His somewhat novel defence at court was that they claimed to be members of the Provisional IRA who were going to kneecap him. His argument was that pretending to be members of a proscribed terrorist organisation rendered his arrest unlawful. This was his lawyer's argument in reality. The defendant was of very low intelligence and slept with his mother, as we discovered when raiding his house one morning. His defence was found to be ridiculous and he was convicted. No police officer would ever act in this way. Even for a laugh.

We once tried a new technique of overt surveillance when following a Northern Irish paedophile. He had been asked to leave Northern Ireland by concerned local citizens in balaclavas, so had moved to London and changed his name. We followed him for most of the day, peeking around corners then ducking back when he turned, talking into our armpits and walking around shops directly behind him. He called 999 on several occasions telling them that he was being followed by the police. A juvenile and silly operation, but at least he wasn't sexually assaulting children or being shot by Republican terrorists.

About an eighth of the Met is made up of CID officers. In this role you attempt to charge people with crimes. If you can't find anyone to charge, you use juju magic and pretend it didn't happen. CID are intellectually superior to uniform officers, and are expected to never leave the building until it's time for the Freemasons' outing to the seaside.

Detectives used to have to get people to admit to a long list of crimes they may or may not know anything about. This practice has ceased until something less obviously open to corruption is found. CID officers used to smoke roll-up cigarettes in the office and start drinking at 1.00pm. These practices have also ceased. The CID used to be an attractive proposition for the hobby drinker who enjoyed fitting up slag, but those days are sadly long gone.

There are a number of specialist detective squads known as 'squads.' The most famous is the Flying Squad. They used to take out old school East End blaggers. Now they are mainly concerned with promising footballers nicking cash from Group 4 trucks before crashing stolen mopeds. Innit.

The murder squad never close a case. They just forget about the ones they haven't solved. The more wooden officers get to go on Crimewatch and say 'Yes Kirsty, that's right,' for no reason. Murders are categorised as A, B or C. Cat C murders are where someone kills someone else then wanders to the police station to tell them all about it. The suspect will be locked up and ready to go before the HAT car is called. The HAT car is the Homicide Assessment Team. They come out and suck their teeth like a cowboy builder before deciding whether the case is glamorous enough for the murder squad. The proximity to the weekend is also a factor when all the detectives will be on double time.

Cat B murders are where the murderer is known, but we don't know where he or she is. They can often be tracked down by someone dressing up as a postman and knocking on the door. If you do it in police uniform they'll hide in the loft. Cat A murders are where the press film everything and the Commissioner has to use a Commander to go on the telly next to the Scotland Yard sign. Nobody will ever have seen this Commander before, so the press can't ask awkward questions about expenses or why he's got blue lights fitted to his Range Rover.

The Counter Terrorism Command used to be the Anti-Terrorist Branch but have softened their media profile in recent years. Their work is covert and highly specialised. Such is the need for secrecy nobody knows what anyone else is doing. Even their mums. They often phone people up but won't say who they are so it is assumed they are selling something and get hung up on. They listen to the police radio when a member of the public reports a suspicious package. They lose interest when the attending officer kicks the package and doesn't lose a leg. Sometimes they speak to foreign people who have been arrested but never use their real names. They got this idea from Spooks *on the telly.*

The Directorate of Professional Standards targets corrupt police officers. Whenever a DPS officer visits a police building everyone sits silently and carefully deletes their Internet history. If the DPS can't gather sufficient evidence to prosecute someone, they will use other methods under the disciplinary code. Hence you will see officers being sacked for having a shit haircut or photocopying their face. The DPS play the long game and consider corporate risk and reputation. DPS officers sleep soundly at night knowing they are not as unpopular as Traffic Officers.

Other specialist units include the helicopter, where it is essential you can talk in a fuzzy upper-class accent. They spend most of their time chasing young inbreds on mopeds across fields. The helicopter does not go up in rain, fog or in the dark. Or on a Sunday morning if the pilot has had a big session the night before. If the helicopter is over west London for more than an hour Heathrow Airport shuts down and everyone gets very upset.

The dog unit is a breed apart. Dogs are chosen following rigorous selection. The real nutters are sent to the army. Some kinder souls apparently decide police work is not for them and are sold to kind people in kind houses. The remainder get to drive around and bite people for running away or hiding in mattresses.

Mounted branch stroll around central London pooing on the road.

The Territorial Support Group are the riot police. They are made up of people who are particularly adept at wearing big riot helmets and standing in lines, occasionally hitting people. In the hierarchy of people who stand in lines, they are number one. They are Level 1 trained which means they can run around with little round shields and break into peoples houses where the occupier is really really not keen on the police. Level 2 officers are one level down from this. They get to wear helmets, but not all the time. Level 3 officers are not allowed to wear riot helmets at all. Level 3 officers wander about aimlessly and get to stand next to police tape. Each group has views on the other — Level 1 officers see themselves as highly trained experts in their field. Other people see them as bellends.

Armed officers come in several versions. You can be in Royalty Protection standing outside Windsor Castle where you have to tell American tourists whether the Queen is at home or not. You need a grey beard to do this job. Stick on beards have been acceptable for female officers since 2012 when they were recognised as an underrepresented group in Royalty Protection. Other armed officers protect diplomatic premises. They stand still for two hours and do not speak to the occupants of their embassy. They are swapped around every two hours to make sure they haven't had a stroke. They also cover Downing Street and every now and then almost cause the Commissioner to resign by alleging a Cabinet Minister called them a pleb.

Officers at airports are given guns, which they use to indicate where Gate 17 is before going for a lie down. Specialist Firearms Officers are top of the tree. They get to drive around in enormous military-like vehicles and wear balaclavas. When they are good, they get to wear their own clothes on a Friday. They get special holsters to carry their guns under their North Face jackets, and side pockets to carry their Andy McNab books in.

Then there is Traffic, who wear white hats so the pigeons know where to aim. They deal with fatal road traffic *collisions and harass innocent motorists. They also make lorry drivers hand over this little plastic disc things which stops them driving for the rest of the day. Traffic is for a certain sort of person.*

When I received my long service medal, each recipient went forward to be presented with the medal by a very senior police officer. Each received a round of applause except the traffic officer who was booed, much to the surprise of his parents. And there were officers from the Directorate of Professional Standards there. Strange world.

The undercover officers had to wear blue blankets over their heads to prevent identification. They had to hold hands and be led up to the stage where they shook hands with the senior officer and had their photos taken. Unusual, but I'm sure you can understand that their safety is paramount — they are also entitled to a free photo like everyone else to mark the momentous day even though they were under a blanket. Like a child molester.

So there it is — The British Police in a nutshell.

Pulling the Pin on the Hand Grenade

The police helicopter thundered above, its spotlight sweeping across the roads and alleyways around us. An industrial estate in west London, early hours of the morning. A teenage boy stabbed, hundreds flee a party, filling the air with shouts and screams.

Some gathered at the end of the road, held back by a line of police dogs. A man stepped forward and kicked one in the head. Bottles smashed at our feet. Information came over the radio that groups of youths were intending to stab a police officer.

I called for more resources to assist in controlling the scene, end the chaos. Unfamiliar officers arrived, asking for direction, and rushed to help others who were becoming overwhelmed.

At the heart of the melee two of my officers administered CPR to the stabbed boy. They too had come under attack and had to request assistance, so they could force their way into the building and try and to save his life. Fortunately, enough officers arrived so we could get the paramedics to the victim safely. And then the ambulance to which he was taken was surrounded and attacked.

Officers fought hand to hand, to force a route through the mob. The officer who accompanied the boy to hospital was set upon by a group who'd followed them when the ambulance got there. One lone figure trying to prevent a hospital from being stormed. Hours later, the morning sun rose over the devastation.

Fuck this, I thought. I was done.

It wasn't just the riot. It was everything. I had lost my sense of humour and, needing to stay in the police for at least twenty-five years to get my gold-plated public sector pension, felt trapped. I couldn't afford to leave, but staying affected me badly.

Corruption was rampant, my team was significantly and dangerously under-resourced and, most importantly, their lives were far too often put at risk. I was no longer in my early-twenties and up for doing stupid dangerous things. Older now, I was also a father and felt parental towards the younger officers. The job was dragging me into dark places.

Then, in March 2017, PC Keith Palmer was murdered by a terrorist. I never met Keith, although we were roughly the same age. He was a father too, an unarmed police officer who gave his life protecting others at the Palace of Westminster.

At the inquest, the Coroner ruled that his death could have been prevented had armed officers been better positioned. They were there but, as always, the unarmed officer was first line of defence. A very senior police officer was present as well. He had no protective equipment or a radio, so locked himself in a car.

That isn't what we do. That *isn't* what a police officer does. I'm sure he had his reasons and other senior officers supported his actions, but I was profoundly angry about that.

In 1994, my fellow training colleague Matthew Parsonson had

died when the car he was in crashed responding to an urgent call for assistance. He had been a policeman for *two weeks* and was going to the aid of another officer who was in grave danger.

Keith Palmer was given CPR by the MP Tobias Ellwood, despite there being genuine fears of a secondary attack.

The locked door. That is what the Met came to represent to me. The *locked* door. I had an unhealthy anger inside me.

Then one night the phone rang at home. It was one of the decent members of the SLT. Yes, what a shocker. Some of them didn't buy into the cabal, and I hoped did the decent thing and reported what was going on. The call was rather unexpected. Us DIs were expected to be available and take them all the time. Until we refused. How angry did the Chief Superintendent get about that! He accused us of disloyalty and all sorts. Just before he headed back to Bramshill to try and get promoted. Again.

Anyway, I assumed something really serious had happened. Instead, it turned out my rather amusing 'Guide to the British Police' had come to the attention of those in high places. They weren't happy and I was ordered to take it down.

I noted the irony of being told my writing wasn't in keeping with the standards expected by a serving police officer by overtly bent coppers. By this stage, I was openly vocal in my opposition to them. I had found a way out and was biding my time, clinging on until I had twenty-five years' service.

'What do those pricks want me to do?' I asked. The caller sounded close to tears, so I agreed to take it down. I would put it straight back up when I resigned I told him. 'I don't really care, Paul,' he said, and I assumed that was the last of it. Obviously not. I was served notice that I was under investigation for bringing the police service into disrepute. Even by the standards of West Area SLT, this was a surprise development. I laughed. So I didn't cry. All the PCs on parade would have been really embarrassed.

I was still under investigation by the IOPC at that point, so felt the weight. I was glad my taking the piss via gentle satire was enough to occupy the forces of local complaint departments and national complaint oversight units. Rather than real corruption. Imagine actually dealing with that!

Given a few weeks to consider my position, I would go only on my own terms. I still had my pride. I was told my writing was offensive to short arses (not in those words, admittedly) and that my mention of women wearing stick-on beards was offensive to women. Suggesting armed police needed a lie down undermined public confidence in policing. 'How many people have actually complained?' I asked. None they said.

'Still getting disciplined though, am I?'

'Yes.'

'What's happening to Paul Martin?'

'In what way?' they asked.

I winked and walked away in a manner they'll never forget.

And then I got door-stepped by the *Mail on Sunday*, who had got wind of how I had been disciplined for trying to be funny. It seemed I had become the first serving police officer ever to be disciplined for writing comedy. This was newsworthy apparently, so they wrote about it. Funny old world.

I decided my time had come and formally notified the Met of my resignation. I wouldn't be able to claim a pension for another two years, but had to go. I was defeated.

I asked to take up the role of Silver Commander for my last three months. I would be based at Hounslow, having oversight of the three Boroughs. We had the highest rate of emergency calls in the Met, I'll have you know, and I would be in charge. A wonderful yet frightening thought – for all of those around me.

I would also be leaving my Ealing response team, which I was sad to do. Many experiences were burned into my memory. I still have the CCTV footage of one officer falling over while racing to an urgent assistance and his accidentally discharged Taser almost hitting a Hammersmith detective. A few weeks before that he and another officer had saved the life of a woman trying to jump off a bridge. They were only there because they got lost en route to another call. Not all heroes wear cloaks. Or carry the London A-Z. The Sergeants activities are worth a book in their own right. If any of them could write, it would be a good idea.

One day I was summonsed to Legal Services in Holborn. They were defending an Employment Tribunal against the Met and Paul Martin personally. The Met fought the action and wanted a statement from me in relation to what had taken place in Southall Police Station and the surrounding circumstances.

I met with a pleasant lawyer and we talked about children's television for a while before getting down to business. I outlined what had gone on and she seemed taken aback. She then asked for my opinion of the various characters involved. Strangely, I felt worried about repercussions. I knew what the boys' club were capable of and was worried about what else they might do.

The lawyer told me it was important they had all the info possible. I could tell her things that would remain confidential between us, but which might sway the direction of the action.

I pulled the pin on the hand grenade* and told her everything, about the corrupt practices, corrupt characters and corrupt stuff that had led to my mental breakdown. She said it sounded like I'd suffered a detriment and intimated I might have grounds for an Employment Tribunal. A huge weight lifted. I was listened to and believed for the first time. I had spent so long being gaslit by the cabal that I half-believed I'd imagined stuff and in fact caused all my own problems. It was only when it was all laid out that I understood fully what had really been going on.

Two days later the Met dropped its defence of the claim and my Southall Acting Sergeant colleague was paid an undisclosed sum in an out of court settlement. I was overjoyed.**

---

* *Not literally.*
** *Literally.*

Working as Silver Commander proved demanding. I missed being able to attend incidents and had to manage everything remotely. I was often the only substantive Inspector on duty, so the demand was huge. Luckily, there was a Greggs within walking distance. Unfortunately, this involved entering Hounslow High Street, which is truly the weirdest place in Britain.

As part of the BCU restructuring, supervision was reduced. I had oversight of an urban area with the same size population as Birmingham, as I think I've mentioned before. I hope you are interested. My line managment wasn't. I wondered how I could offer any sort of supervision and support to roughly one hundred officers on a shift-by-shift basis. So I left it to the Sergeants. Some had passed the Inspector exam. Although not substantive in rank, they were substantial in girth. I didn't get where I am today by not delegating responsibility.

Expected to lie about staffing levels, as I was approaching my leaving date, I was even less likely to fiddle figures than I was as a DI. Once, I told Scotland Yard that we were so short-staffed the situation was critical. I then got a call from Paul Martin who kept calling himself Mr Martin like a pretentious actor using the third person. He actually growled at me. Seriously. He growled down the phone. I assumed he was threatening me. It wasn't the first time. He demanded I count people off sick in the figures because he knew they were lying. 'Takes one to know one,' I said, but the growls may have drowned me out.

One shift, we had two fatal simultaneous stabbings, a couple of young men murdered in separate incidents. I used to manage my emotions by finding reasons why the victims were not like my own children. A way of ensuring I believed such things could not happen to them. I imagined the victims had died due to their lifestyle choices, criminal records, places they lived, people they hung around with. Not this time.

The second victim was the same age as my oldest son. He was at a train station, travelling to watch a football match. Just as my own son often did. A man on the opposite platform decided he was looking at him, so crossed over and stabbed him in the chest.

The victim had lived nearby. His father went to the station and saw police and paramedics carrying out CPR on his boy. He watched his 20-year-old son die. The lad's mother worked for the police. I couldn't imagine the pain they were suffering.

Soon, in October 2019, my last week as a police officer in the Metropolitan Police Service arrived. I had been there twenty-five years. I asked to be taken off shift work, but this was refused by the SLT; an unsurprising development. My last shift would be on night duty. They told me I was going to be put onto twelve-hour shifts the following week. I emailed to say how sorry I was, but I was taking early retirement that week. They could therefore place the twelve-hour shifts somewhere without sunshine.

My last shift began and Sergeants from the three Boroughs came to see me off, shake my hand and say goodbye. I was moved by this. My old team had a whip round and got me some gifts and a card, which I was presented with at my retirement drink-a-thon a few weeks later. I had some wonderful messages from them, with very little profanity. I still miss that team a lot. If you ever get nicked in Ealing, please say hi from Paul.

I heard nothing from the Senior Leadership Team or wider Met, however, despite having given twenty-five years of my life to an organisation that broke me. There wasn't even an email of acknowledgement. I'd been spat out. The sad thing is I wasn't really surprised. I didn't believe in any of it anymore.

At 3.00am, I handed my warrant card to the Control Room Sergeant, shook his hand, and left Hounslow Police Station by the rear doors. It was over. It was all fucking over.

I couldn't control my emotions. Tears streaming down my face, I got to my car in a nearby car park and sat there for a few minutes. I wasn't a police officer anymore. I had left the job that had defined my life. Policing had built me up, made me the person I was – and destroyed me.

I'd planned to drive to Shepherd's Bush, to Askew Road, where I'd seen the two women die in a burning building all those years before. I wanted to say sorry and to try and start to forget. Then I paused. I wouldn't go. I would keep their memory alive by not trying to forget about them. It was the least I could do.

I played 'After All' by The Frank and Walters and drove home through the dark deserted streets of West Area. I got home and must have made enough noise to wake up my wife. I sat on the sofa drinking beer in the dark. She called down, asking if I was okay.

'Yes. Yes I am,' I said.

Two weeks after I left the Met in October 2019, the Directorate of Professional Standards moved against Paul Martin and his crew. They were moved to other roles in the police, pending the outcome of the investigation against them.

On my birthday weekend in January 2022, Paul Martin and Davinder 'Ricky' Kandohla were sacked from the Metropolitan Police Service. Here's what the Met had to say:

> *Two Metropolitan Police officers have been dismissed following an investigation by the Met's Directorate of Professional Standards.*
>
> *A misconduct hearing, led by an Independent Legally Qualified Chair, concluded on Sunday 16 January, with all findings and sanctions being read into public record.*
>
> *Chief Superintendent Paul Martin was found to have breached Standards of Professional Behaviour, amounting to gross misconduct, in relation to honesty and integrity, orders and instructions, duties and responsibilities, authority, respect and courtesy, and equality and diversity.*

The breaches related to, misusing a corporate credit card, conduct towards more junior members of staff including a pregnant colleague and failing to declare a conflict of interest while assisting in a promotion process for Chief Inspector Davinder Kandohla.

He was dismissed without notice.

Chief Inspector Kandohla was also found to have breached Standards of Professional Behaviour amounting to gross misconduct, in relation to honesty and integrity, authority, respect and courtesy, duties and responsibilities and discreditable conduct.

The breaches related to failing to declare a conflict of interest while taking part in his own promotion process, providing a misleading account to professional standards officers during an investigation into expenses he had claimed and conduct towards junior members of staff.

He was dismissed without notice.

The hearing also considered allegations against two other officers.

Sergeant James Di-Luzio was found to have breached Standards of Professional Behaviour, amounting to misconduct, in relation to, orders and instructions, duties and responsibilities, and authority, respect and courtesy.

The breaches related to the misuse of a corporate credit card and conduct towards more junior members of staff.

He was issued with management advice.

Commander Catherine Roper said: "The behaviour demonstrated by these officers has no place in the Met. It is right they have been subject to a detailed and thorough investigation by the DPS, resulting in a misconduct hearing and the subsequent sanctions.

"Three of the officers were of a leadership rank and should have been setting a strong example for the standards we hold in the Met. Instead they abused their trusted positions; in particular in the way they spoke to and treated more junior members of staff was appalling. This behaviour will not be tolerated by anyone in the Met and we will continue to investigate and hold to account those who act in this manner."

Too little. Too late. It was tolerated far too long and seems still to be going on. Police corruption is like electricity, everywhere, but you only notice it when you stick a proverbial finger in the socket. Over and out.

Acknowledgements

To Arthur Smith, the Legend of Comedy, for encouraging and supporting my journey into the world of creativity and performance.

Also to Sofia Cann for her endless encouragement and for making this book become reality.

Investigate our other titles and
stay up to date with all our latest releases at
www.scratchingshedpublishing.co.uk